# Women of the Church

**WHAT EVERY CATHOLIC SHOULD KNOW**

# Women of the Church

## WHAT EVERY CATHOLIC SHOULD KNOW

Bronwen McShea

With a Foreword by
Patricia Snow

IGNATIUS PRESS
San Francisco

AUGUSTINE INSTITUTE
Greenwood Village, CO

Cover art
*Mary Going to the Temple, Four Female Saints,
and a Female Donor and her Daughter* (detail)
Unidentified artist, 15th century
Courtesy of
The Barnes Foundation, Philadelphia
Image in the public domain

Cover design by Kirk Flory

*For Colleen, Elizabeth, Kelley,*
*Emma, Evelyn, Fiona, Tara, and Felicity*

# CONTENTS

# Acknowledgments

I am grateful to everyone at Ignatius Press and the Augustine Institute who had a hand in bringing this book into being, especially Father Joseph Fessio, S.J., Mark Brumley, Diane Eriksen, Kathy Mosier, Kris Gray, Madelynn Felix, Joseph Pearce, and Christopher Blum.

My colleague Elizabeth Klein and my friends Patricia Siedlecki Zinsser, Father Sam Conedera, S.J., Marion Boteju, Colin Moran, and Kimberly Woodard were supportive in a variety of critical ways throughout the period I was laboring over this book.

Foundational for the book were my interactions with students in my Augustine Institute master's course Women of the Church, which I taught in 2020 and 2022, and with undergraduate and graduate students in my course Women in Europe, 1300–1800, which I taught for the history department at the University of Nebraska Omaha in 2017. Opportunities to engage with audiences in lectures and talks sponsored by Saint John's University, Legatus Denver, Legatus Fairfield County, the Thomistic Institute in New York City, and the Merton Institute at Columbia University also helped me refine the book in the final stages.

An array of wonderful scholars and teachers over the years, including Carlos Eire and Louis Miller, led me to some of the figures, historical contexts, and sources I touch on in this book. And various friends and acquaintances with whom I interact on social media kindly brought several of the lesser-known women mentioned in this book to my attention.

Patricia Snow was generous not only in writing this book's foreword but also in offering extensive feedback on my original manuscript. Patricia is also among a number of Catholic women who have modeled Christian womanhood to me and blessed my life beyond measure. This group includes more than I can name, but I wish to give special mention to my mother, Maureen McGowan McShea, who was also my first teacher and who introduced me as a girl to many of the saints and other historical personalities covered in this book. With appreciation, too, for ways other women in my family strive to live the faith and ensure its transmission to the next generations—and with the hope that my scholarship and writing is of some use to them in that endeavor—I have dedicated this book to my sister Colleen McShea, my sisters-in-law Elizabeth Purdy McShea and Kelley Myers McShea, and my beloved nieces, Emma, Evelyn, Fiona, Tara, and Felicity McShea.

# Foreword

*By Patricia Snow*

Bronwen McShea, a historian by training, has written a small but comprehensive book about Catholic women, which is organized chronologically, beginning with Mary of Nazareth and ending with Mother Teresa's Missionaries of Charity. While most surveys of Catholic women focus exclusively on female saints, McShea has cast a wider net, including brief biographies of more complicated figures, such as Isabella of Castile, the patroness of Christopher Columbus, who, even as she persecuted Muslims and Jews in fifteenth-century Spain, undertook extensive reforms of corrupt Catholic institutions in advance of the provocations of Protestantism.

For readers like me, whose grasp of history is unsure, McShea provides a clarifying overview. She gives us women in context, in particularized settings, responding both to large-scale historical movements and local emerging needs. In the framework of the book, all the familiar historical periods fall into place (the Renaissance, the Enlightenment), and as a bonus, many common identifiers such as the Patristic Era, the Hundred Years' War, the word *Christendom*, and so on are succinctly defined, bringing welcome clarity where, for many of us, a certain vagueness prevailed.

As the book's chronology unfolds, so does its cast of characters. Queens and freed slaves, administrators and mystics, educators, foundresses, nurses, missionaries—the vocations pile up, begging the question why any woman would complain of being excluded from the priesthood, but also raising the question whether there are any generalizations to be drawn about what John Paul II called the feminine genius.

Two generalizations, at least, can be hazarded. First, while reading the book, one cannot but be struck by how *relational* its heroines are, how gifted at forging and sustaining the kinds of relationships that are essential to communities and also at encouraging, often behind the scenes, the more visible vocations of prominent, socially powerful men. In the early centuries of Christianity, when women's social mobility was limited, their ecclesial relationships were often literally familial: maternal, in the cases of Saints Helena and Monica; sororal, in the case of Saint Macrina the Younger, who oversaw the spiritual development of her brothers Saints Basil the Great and Gregory of Nyssa; or uxorial, in the case of Saint Clotilde, who shepherded her pagan husband into the Church. Far more than the other way around, we read of early Christian women praying fervently for the conversions of their husbands and sons, exhibiting from the beginning a gift for intercessory prayer, the same gift Saints Francis of Assisi and Dominic would recognize and harness centuries later when they established communities of contemplative women to undergird their work in the world.

This female gift for relationships also manifested in the Church's history as a gift for friendship: the friendship of Saint Phoebe for Saint Paul, or Saint Marcella for Saint Jerome. In the same way that a group of women accompanied Jesus in His lifetime and ministered to His followers, a certain kind of devout woman has always nurtured and supported the life of the Church by befriending her priests, embracing their congregations, and even providing physical spaces for the Church to assemble, including in cellars and barns in martyrdom-risking periods of persecution.

In time, as women's opportunities expanded, so did their distinctive ministries of upbuilding and encouragement. Far from abandoning such work, Catholic women began practicing it on a larger scale, making the transition, for example, from praying for missionaries to becoming missionaries themselves, or from being the benefactresses of Jesuit schools for boys to founding congregations dedicated to the education of girls. "I loved a child as we should love / Each other everywhere," Rose Hawthorne Lathrop wrote in the aftermath of her only child's death, as she began to envision a ministry to the cancerous poor.[1] In the same spirit in the modern era, communities of Catholic women worldwide have ministered to the marginal and the indigent, the sick and the dying, lending credence to John Paul II's observation that, as God entrusted Jesus to Mary, he has entrusted the human being to women in a special way.

This entrusting, however, should not be understood sentimentally. The work of a mother or older sister is always spiritual as well as corporeal and always includes the weighty responsibilities of correcting and admonishing. When Thérèse of Lisieux, in the process of discerning her vocation, declared, "In the heart of the Church ... I will be Love," the kind of love to which she was referring was not indulgent but fierce, as "strong as death", in the words of the Song of Songs (8:6), and always willing the ultimate good of the other.[2] Shouldering the responsibilities of this kind of love, many Catholic women, in times of ecclesial crisis, have emerged as the galvanizing conscience of the larger Church, speaking truth to the power of imperial Rome, in the case of the virgin martyrs, or urging the diffident, ultimately treacherous Charles VII to his coronation, in the case of Joan of Arc. Not only in the consequential public ministries of a Catherine of Siena or a Dorothy Day, but also in the most ordinary Catholic families, we

---

1    Patricia Dunlavy Valenti, *To Myself a Stranger: A Biography of Rose Hawthorne* (Baton Rouge, LA: Louisiana State University Press, 1991), 90.
2    John Beevers, trans., *The Autobiography of Saint Thérèse of Lisieux: The Story of a Soul* (New York: Image Books, 2001), 161.

so often see the same dynamic in place: the mother upholding the higher standard; the woman as the moral center and conscience of the family.

The second generalization we might draw about the feminine genius concerns woman's *receptivity*, a receptivity grounded in biology, in the sexual act by which human beings become co-creators with God. In sexual intercourse, man gives and woman receives; man generates life outside himself, while woman conceives it within, sheltering and nourishing it until it is strong enough to be delivered to the world. Secular feminism, so averse to passivity, strongly resists the implications of this biological reality, associating passivity with victimhood and the wrong kind of sacrifice—with the "burnt offering" of Psalm 51:16, for example, a kind of sacrifice that God does indeed refuse. But if it is true, as Gertrud von Le Fort insisted, that "surrender to God is the only absolute power that the creature possesses", and moreover that "the passive acceptance inherent in woman ... appears in the Christian order of grace as the positively decisive factor", it follows that in the work of becoming fully human, woman has a certain natural advantage over man, who, his role in procreation notwithstanding, is, after all, also a human being and so also has to learn, by a more counterintuitive catechesis, the necessity of surrendering himself, receiving God's love interiorly, and bearing its fruit in the world.[3]

What modernity resists as a negative, in other words, the Church has always affirmed as a gift: a gift for hearing and receiving, absorbing and remembering. The importance of the gift and its privileged association with femininity may explain why, when divine messages have been delivered to the human race, they have so often been entrusted to women, and even to

---

3   Gertrud von Le Fort, *The Eternal Woman: The Timeless Meaning of the Feminine*, trans. Marie Cecilia Buehrle (San Francisco: Ignatius Press, 2010), 9, 18.

young girls. It is as if, when the survival of such messages has been at stake, the good soil of the female heart has outweighed woman's disadvantaged social status, including her often compromised credibility. So many of the women in McShea's book are the spiritual descendants of Mary Magdalene: favored recipients of divine revelations, or *showings*, as Julian of Norwich called them. When God has wanted a medal struck or an image painted, Christ's Sacred Heart venerated or His Divine Mercy better understood, or when He has wished to impress upon us the supreme importance of doing even small things with great love, or of recognizing His Son in the distressing disguise of the poor, all these and similar burdens He has placed on female hearts. And the women He has chosen—Saints Catherine Labouré and Faustina Kowalska, Saints Margaret Mary Alacoque and Catherine of Genoa, Saints Gertrude, Bridget, Teresa of Avila, and countless others—have labored indefatigably to convey His messages to the world, bearing with misunderstanding and ridicule, incomprehension and envy, and even accusations of mendacity, mental illness, and heresy.

In the case of the most urgent messages, or warnings, the female principle has intensified. In places like Fátima, warnings about impending judgment and the reality of Hell have come to (mostly) young girls *from* a woman, from Mary, whose Annunciation submission remains the prototype of all human surrender. And if the response Mary has requested is the same intercessory prayer at which women have excelled from the beginning, she has not asked us in these late apparitions to pray for family and friends, particular missions, or cherished communities. As the woman moves to the center and the dimensions of the female project become clear, we have been asked to pray for all human beings without exception, for the conversion of sinners, and for the salvation of the world.

# Preface

Some years ago, I was blessed to spend several days in Assisi, Italy, where a Franciscan friar gave me a tour of the Convent of San Damiano. Built in the twelfth century, San Damiano was the home of Saint Clare of Assisi and the first women to join her as religious sisters.

I saw many wonderful things that day. Yet my strongest memories include sitting on a bench where Saint Clare often sat while taking her meals and touching stones upon which her sisters spent hard hours washing linens and garments by hand.

I was struck, in short, by the ordinary humanity that one of the most celebrated saints in the history of the Catholic Church shared with me and all who prepare meals and do laundry.

When I was a girl and first receiving the Catholic faith from my parents, I learned about remarkable female saints such as Clare, Catherine of Siena, Bernadette of Lourdes, and of course our Blessed Mother. As I grew up, however, I noticed a pattern with respect to the figures in the Church's history to whom I was most drawn. Most were men, not women. And I was drawn to them—Saint Augustine of Hippo, Saint Thomas More, Jesuit missionaries who crisscrossed the globe—because of how dynamic they seemed. Books, films, and works of art to which I was exposed reinforced the view that the great women of the Church were fewer than the men and that they were less interesting and relatable too.

It was not until I was in graduate school that I began to realize my error. That error was owed, it turned out, to the way the history of the Church and the stories of the saints had typically been written and transmitted to ordinary Catholics. For a variety of reasons, there were wide gaps between what I had learned in my American Catholic upbringing about women in the Church and what scholars knew—and are still coming to know and appreciate—about the great diversity and complexity of countless women who for two millennia have been at the heart of the Church's life and have been shaping history just as much as the men.

At Yale, for example, I was exposed to Saint Teresa of Avila's autobiography, which moved me as much as Augustine's *Confessions* had earlier. I also became familiar with specialized research on fascinating Catholic women, canonized and not, of Teresa's era. I read the *Relations de la Nouvelle-France* by Jesuits who had worked alongside Saint Isaac Jogues and the other North American martyrs, and I learned how crucial Native American and French women were to the growth of the Church in the seventeenth century, including Saints Kateri Tekakwitha and Marie de l'Incarnation.

As I learned about many remarkable Catholic women of past times, I wondered how my own development might have been different had there been more and better resources available to my parents and other teachers who labored to pass down to me my patrimony as a daughter of the Church.

I have written this book for Catholic readers of all ages as a shortcut to stories about women of the Church that took me years to learn and piece together on my own. This book features not only well-known saints but also many other women—canonized, beatified, awaiting beatification, and at times important historically but not deserving of veneration—whom I believe every Catholic should know.

But this book is also for anyone interested in the history of Catholicism—to demonstrate that the history of the Church's women *is the Church's history*, just as much as the history of her men is.

As this book is part of a series, it could only be so long. Some readers will feel I have not given enough space to this or that beloved figure. Some may also notice that I have devoted considerable space to Catholic women of the early modern period. This stems from my specialized historical training and expertise, which I am grateful to share with my fellow Catholics. I ask all readers not to regard this book as my definitive take on the importance of various figures but to accept it as the fruit of my study of the Church's history up to now and as a road map to further reading.

Recalling again my visit to Assisi, I ask my readers, too, to remain mindful that each woman covered in this book was, and remains even if she is in Heaven, as human as Clare of Assisi was when eating bread and soup or making sure laundry was done on schedule. Each was as real and ordinary as we are. Where ordinary women have achieved remarkable things for God and the Church, it has been because God loved them enough to become human like them—to share with them the life of His divine and human Son, through His Jewish mother, Mary, in real, historical time. God worked with their particular frailties and potentialities—purifying and elevating them and uniting them to Himself. By His grace, He made them—as He does the whole Church and all that He redeems in creation—*more truly themselves*, more wonderfully what He intended them to be, from and for all eternity.

## Chapter 1

# The Apostolic and Patristic Era

Toward the end of the reign of the Roman emperor Tiberius, a Jewish woman named Mary (*Maryam* in Aramaic) stood at the foot of a cross outside the walls of Jerusalem, watching her beloved Son, Jesus (*Yeshua*, as she knew Him), suffer and die as if He were a common criminal. According to the Gospel of Saint John the Apostle, Jesus said to Mary before He died, "Woman, behold, your son", while gesturing toward young John. He then said to John, "Behold, your mother."[1]

Mary and John would remember these words of Jesus in the coming days, reflecting on their meaning. After the miracles of the Lord's Resurrection, His Ascension into Heaven, and the descent of the Holy Spirit, the followers of Jesus began to address Mary as "Mother". Mary, who came from the small town of Nazareth in Judaea, would in time be revered not only as the mother of *the Christos*, of *the Savior*, of *God's own Son*, but also as the mother of *His whole Church*—the body of those gathering in His name and looking forward to eternal life in His heavenly kingdom.

### Mary of Nazareth, Mother of the Church

Despite obscure origins, Mary of Nazareth is the most famous woman in all of history. Christians have claimed from the

---

1   Jn 19:26–27.

earliest centuries of the Church that she gave birth to Jesus as a virgin, that she was sinless, and that she was miraculously assumed into Heaven at the end of her earthly life. She is prayed to in every language. Every day, priests, religious, and laypeople throughout the world pray Rosaries to her and, in the Liturgy of the Hours, recite the Magnificat— a set of verses attributed to Mary when she was pregnant with Jesus:

> My soul proclaims the greatness of the Lord, my spirit rejoices in God my Savior, for He has looked with favor on His lowly servant. From this day all generations will call me blessed. The Almighty has done great things for me, and holy is His Name. He has mercy on those who fear Him in every generation. He has shown the strength of his arm. He has scattered the proud in their conceit. He has cast down the mighty from their thrones and has lifted up the lowly. He has filled the hungry with good things, and the rich He has sent away empty. He has come to the help of His servant Israel, for He has remembered His promise of mercy, the promise He made to our fathers, to Abraham and his children forever.[2]

Countless books have been written about—and controversies have erupted over—Mary's precise relationship to her Son, to God the Father, to God the Holy Spirit, to all Christians, and to the whole of creation. She has been depicted in every artistic medium in lifelike, masterful, rustic, crude, and symbolic ways. Innumerable hymns and songs have been composed in her honor. For example, the *Akathist to the Theotokos*, a sixth-century Greek hymn, salutes the Mother of God with these verses:

---

2   *Christian Prayer: The Liturgy of the Hours* (New York: Christian Book Publishing, 1976), 696.

Rejoice, the Restoration of fallen Adam.
Rejoice, the Redemption of the tears of Eve.
Rejoice, O Height beyond human logic.
Rejoice, O depth invisible even to the eyes of Angels.
Rejoice, for you are the King's throne.
Rejoice, you bear Him, Who bears the universe.[3]

A late-sixteenth-century German Christmas carol poetically honors Mary's giving birth to Jesus:

Lo, how a Rose e'er blooming
From tender stem hath sprung!
Of Jesse's lineage coming,
As men of old have sung.

And a traditional African American spiritual includes these lines:

Sister Mary had-a but one child
Born in Bethlehem.
And-a every time-a the-a baby cried,
She'd a-rocked Him in the weary land.[4]

Mary of Nazareth, who offered Christ maternal comfort and wisdom at every stage of His earthly life—including in the darkest hours of His Passion and Death—is the *preeminent woman*. Without her willing embrace of the mission God asked of her, the Church would have no history.

She was chosen to be, and *chose to be*, the archetypal woman of the Church—the only one of the "living stones" that Christ

---

3    David M. Gwynn, *Christianity in the Later Roman Empire: A Sourcebook* (London: Bloomsbury, 2014), 92.
4    Roland Hayes, *My Favorite Spirituals: 30 Songs for Voice and Piano* (Mineola, NY: Dover Publications, 2001), 98.

employed while building His Church from which He Himself, the Church's Cornerstone, was hewn.[5] She modeled fidelity, patience, perseverance, hope, and love to all Christ's first disciples. And from Heaven she has given motherly comfort and strength to the whole Church ever since.

Mary also helped gather numerous other women who were among the first disciples. They, too, became mothers of the Church in their own ways. In the Gospel of Luke, we read that as Christ traveled through various towns and cities, women accompanied Him alongside the Twelve Apostles. Among them were Mary Magdalene; Joanna, the wife of King Herod's steward Chuza; a woman named Susanna; and many others who nurtured Christ's mission with their presence and means.[6]

### Mary Magdalene, Apostle to the Apostles

Saint Mary Magdalene, who witnessed Christ's Crucifixion, too, is also one of the most famous women in history. The Gospel writers referred to her by name more than they did some of the Twelve. Probably a woman of wealth who hailed from Magdala in Judaea, she was, according to Saint Luke, a person plagued by demons that Christ drove out of her.[7]

Centuries after she lived, preachers and artists began identifying her with the unnamed woman in Luke 7, who anointed Christ's feet and may have been a repentant prostitute. Regardless, the Church has always acknowledged that she was close to Christ. As the Gospels attest, He appeared to her first on Easter morning and charged her with telling the initially incredulous Apostles about His Resurrection.

---

5    1 Pet 2:5; see Eph 2:20.
6    See Lk 8:1–3.
7    Ibid.

For this reason, there is a tradition in the Church, dating to the eleventh century and affirmed in the thirteenth by Saint Thomas Aquinas, of honoring Mary Magdalene as *apostolorum apostola* (apostle to the apostles).[8] In his *Commentary on the Gospel of John*, Aquinas said:

> Notice the three privileges given to Mary Magdalene. First, she had the privilege of being a prophet (*propheticum*) because she was worthy enough to see the angels.... Secondly, she had the dignity or rank of an angel (*angelorum fastigium*) insofar as she looked upon Christ.... Thirdly, she had the office of an apostle (*officium apostolicum*); indeed, she was an apostle to the apostles (*immo facta est apostolorum apostola*) insofar as it was her task to announce our Lord's resurrection to the disciples. Thus ... it was a woman who would be the first to announce the words of life.[9]

### Phoebe, Priscilla, and Thecla, friends of Paul

Just as Mary the Mother of God, Mary Magdalene, and other women such as Mary and Martha of Bethany were crucial to Christ's ministry while He walked the earth, women helped build up the Church in her first decades after Christ's Ascension. The Acts of the Apostles, the letters of Saint Paul, and other early Christian sources give ample testimony of this.

Paul himself depended upon women as his ministry developed after his dramatic conversion on the road to Damascus. Among them was Saint Phoebe, a prominent woman in the young Christian community at Cenchreae, near the Greek

---

8    Michelle A. Erhardt and Amy M. Morris, eds., *Mary Magdalene, Iconographic Studies from the Middle Ages to the Baroque* (Leiden, NL: Brill, 2012), 102, 248n.

9    Quoted in Randall B. Smith, *Aquinas, Bonaventure, and the Scholastic Culture of Medieval Paris: Preaching, Prologues, and Biblical Commentary* (Cambridge, UK: Cambridge University Press, 2021), 210.

city of Corinth. Paul entrusted his Letter to the Romans to her and at one point referred to her as a "deaconess", although scholars debate what this meant to first-century people.[10] Regardless, it is partly to Phoebe that we owe the transmission and survival of a critical New Testament book.

Paul also referred in Romans to Saints Priscilla and Aquila, a Jewish woman and her husband who risked their lives to help his work. One of the first Christian churches was in their home. Paul expressed the thanks that "all the churches of the Gentiles" owed them.[11]

Saint Thecla was another celebrated woman associated with Paul. The second-century text *The Acts of Paul and Thecla* gives details about her. Thecla was a pagan noblewoman from Iconium (present-day Konya, Turkey) who, while engaged to be married, heard Paul's teachings on holy virginity. She was moved to dedicate her life to the Christian God. Angering her mother and her fiancé when she ended her engagement, she escaped their efforts to arrest her and left with Paul for Antioch. There, Thecla successfully fought off an attempted rapist but was put on trial for assaulting him. She was saved yet again, this time from execution, reportedly by miraculous means.

Thecla ended up living a long life, sharing the Good News about Christ with others, encouraging other women to devote themselves radically to God, engaging in a healing ministry, and possibly dying as a martyr. Over the centuries, many churches, religious communities, and even cities were dedicated to her, including a monastery in Cyprus established by another convert, Saint Helena.

Helena's conversion, like Paul's, would be one of the most consequential in history. It would not take place, however,

---

10  Rom 16:1.
11  Rom 16:3–4.

until the end of a terrible period of persecution of Christians in the Roman Empire—one in which many women would bravely give their lives in fidelity to God.

### The women martyrs of the early Church

The first Roman emperor who targeted Christians was Nero. According to the historian Tacitus, Nero scapegoated them for a great fire that raged in the city of Rome for over a week in July A.D. 64. Nero had started the blaze himself, it was rumored, to clear away areas of the city so he could begin constructing new buildings and monuments, including a palace for himself. The Christians were an easy target for deflecting the blame, as their worship of a crucified Jewish carpenter and their aversion to various Roman customs marginalized them already in Roman society. Christian women, men, and children were crucified, thrown to hungry beasts before jeering crowds, and burned alive. Paul's friends Priscilla and Aquila were probably among them.

The persecution of Christians intensified, especially under Emperor Marcus Aurelius a century later. Among those killed in this period was fifteen-year-old Saint Blandina, a slave imprisoned in 177 by a military commander in Lugdunum (present-day Lyon, France) in the Roman province of Gaul.

According to a document cited in the fourth century by Eusebius of Caesarea, the Church's first historian, Blandina faced questioning by Roman officials with remarkable bravery. She also encouraged other Christians to remain steadfast in insisting on their innocence when accused of heinous things such as cannibalism and incest. Blandina then withstood a brutal round of torture in an amphitheater. After refusing to accept the Roman gods as her own—which would have ended her bodily suffering—she was stabbed to death after being scourged, burned on a heated grate, and attacked by a steer.[12]

The most famous female martyrs of the early Church include Saints Perpetua and Felicity, who were killed in Roman Carthage in North Africa most likely in 203. Perpetua was a young married noblewoman who was nursing a newborn when she was imprisoned around age twenty-two. Felicity was Perpetua's slave and was pregnant when she, too, was thrown into prison.

A contemporaneous text, *The Passion of Perpetua and Felicity*, indicates that the two young women were arrested for their Christian faith, together with several men, by the local governor, Hilarianus, who saw this as a fitting birthday tribute to Emperor Septimius Severus. Everyone in the group was preparing for baptism. Facing likely execution, Perpetua was tempted to renounce Christ when her father, who did not understand her faith, urged her to do so for her infant's sake.[13]

Perpetua, Felicity, and their companions were attacked in the local amphitheater by an angry cow and a leopard. When the animals did not kill them, the crowd demanded their death by the sword. The guards present obliged. Felicity had only days before given birth to a daughter while in prison. In her case, the crowd witnessed a young woman slain while her breasts, exposed during the violence, dripped with milk. Given the life-giving power symbolized by the new mother's milk and blood, the image of Felicity's martyrdom is the most powerful in the corpus of early Christian writings.[14]

Older women also gave their lives for Christ during the Roman persecutions. Saints Callinica and Basilissa, for

---

12  Paul L. Maier, ed., *Eusebius—The Church History: A New Translation with Commentary* (Grand Rapids, MI: Kregel Publications, 1999), 172–77.

13  Bernard Green, *Christianity in Ancient Rome: The First Three Centuries* (London: T&T Clark, 2010), 132–33.

14  Monica Migliorino Miller, *The Authority of Women in the Catholic Church* (Steubenville, OH: Emmaus Road Publishing, 2015), 163.

example, were two wealthy married women living in Asia Minor who risked their safety to supply food and other necessities to fellow Christians imprisoned during the reign of Emperor Decius. They were arrested in 252 and, after refusing to offer sacrifices to Roman idols, were tortured and decapitated.[15]

Persecutions of Christians continued to flare up throughout the Roman Empire until the early fourth century, especially during the reign of Emperor Diocletian, which lasted from 284 to 305. Saints Lucy of Syracuse and Agnes of Rome, who both suffered greatly defending their virginity against cruel pagan men, were killed in this period, as were the martyrs Saints Margaret of Antioch and Catherine of Alexandria.

Although the historicity of Margaret and Catherine is in doubt among modern scholars, both traditionally have eminent places in the martyrologies of the Eastern and Western churches. Margaret, according to the primary tradition about her, was a young girl from Pisidia in Asia Minor who, after losing her mother quite young, was raised by a group of Christian women and dedicated her virginity to God. Around 304, when she was a teenager, a local Roman official sought to marry her and insisted she renounce Christianity. He had her tortured and killed when she refused.

Catherine was long regarded to have been the scholarly daughter of a Roman governor in the Egyptian city of Alexandria, and one who was convinced to embrace Christianity after receiving a vision of the Blessed Virgin and the Child Jesus. As persecutions of Christians were ongoing during the reign of the eastern Roman emperor, Maxentius (after Diocletian had divided the empire in half), Catherine is believed to have approached Maxentius to ask him to stop the persecutions,

---

15. Agnes B. C. Dunbar, *A Dictionary of Saintly Women*, 2 vols. (London: George Bell & Sons, 1904–1905), 1:141.

only to be interrogated by pagan scholars and condemned to death. Catherine's symbol is a spiked wheel, which was employed in an attempt to kill her, but which shattered when she touched it. She was beheaded instead, but only after others were inspired by her to become Christians too.

### Helena, mother of Emperor Constantine the Great

When Maxentius became the eastern Roman emperor, there was confusion and strife over the eastern and western empires' possible reunification by whichever Roman leader could assert the power to achieve it. The man who eventually restored peace to this situation, Constantine the Great, also dramatically altered the course of the Church's history by legalizing Christianity across his vast domains.

Constantine's decision to protect the Church, and eventually to embrace Christianity himself, was due to the influence of his mother, Helena. But years before her son rose to a position of significance, she was an obscure young Greek woman with no idea of what lay in store.

Born into a humble family around 248 in Bithynia in Asia Minor, Flavia Julia Helena probably worked in an inn or a stable when she was in her teens. A turning point came when she met a young Roman general, Flavius Constantius, who also was of humble origins but who had risen up the ranks of the Roman army while serving Emperor Aurelian. The two became lovers. It is unclear whether they married.

Around 272, Helena gave birth to Constantius' son Flavius Valerius Constantinus. While this boy—the future Constantine the Great—was growing up, his father's star rose further. Emperor Diocletian made him a prefect with powers in the western areas of the empire where the Romans were fighting Germanic tribes. Not long after this, Constantius discarded Helena so he could marry the noblewoman Theodora, who was the daughter of Maximian, Diocletian's son and coemperor in the east. But he ensured that young Constantine, then training as a soldier, was given a high place in Diocletian's court.

Brokenhearted, Helena stayed close to her son, who became a capable commander of troops in war zones and one of the most eminent men in the empire—especially after his father briefly succeeded Diocletian as the western emperor. Then, in 306, when several Roman leaders were vying for control over two halves of the empire, Helena saw her son proclaimed as his father's successor by the army in the west.

This put Constantine at odds with the eastern emperor, Galerius, and the son of Maximian, Maxentius. Both rejected Constantine's right to rule in the west and were persecuting Christians. After a period of civil war—one in which Maxentius attacked Constantine by calling Helena a prostitute—Constantine's forces, despite being vastly outnumbered, defeated Maxentius' at the Battle of the Milvian Bridge north of Rome on October 28, 312.

By this point, Helena had converted to Christianity. She became devoted to penitence and prayer, and her son developed a sympathy for Christians. Indeed, according to an early Christian source, Constantine had an unusual dream prior to the Battle of the Milvian Bridge that inspired him to order his troops to put a Christian symbol—the overlapping Greek letters chi and rho—on their shields before going into battle. The historian Eusebius later claimed that before the battle, Constantine also saw a cruciform light in the sky with the message *In hoc signo vinces* ("In this sign, you will conquer"). Constantine favored his mother's faith and her fellow Christians ever more as the years passed. Indeed, he ended the long period of persecution by issuing the Edict of Milan in 313, legalizing Christianity across the empire.

Once Constantine was fully in power, he gave Helena a place of honor at court. She was also permitted to use public funds to go on a pilgrimage to Palestine to find Christian relics. Helena used some of these funds to support the Church of the Nativity in Bethlehem and the Church of Eleona on the Mount of Olives. There is an ancient tradition that Helena had a temple to the Roman goddess Venus destroyed when she learned it had been constructed at the site of Christ's tomb. And legend has it that, during an excavation near the site, the crosses of Christ and the two thieves executed with Him were unearthed and that, upon hearing this news, Constantine, with his mother's encouragement, ordered the construction of the great Church of the Holy Sepulchre that still stands.

Helena brought pieces of the cross believed to be Christ's back to Rome and spent her last years dedicated to both Christianity and her son's reign. She died around 330 with Constantine nearby. Although she did not live to see him fully embrace Christianity, she did witness his unprecedented convening of an ecumenical council of the Church, the First Council of Nicaea, in 325. At Nicaea, he was determined to see the Church's bishops, who were squabbling over divergent understandings of Christ's relationship to God the Father, settle on a common creed. Catholics have professed this creed ever since.

Constantine, Pope Sylvester I, and other leading churchmen rightly have received the credit for Nicaea I. However, we may wonder how differently the Church's entire history might have played out had Constantine been raised by a different mother than Helena, whose remarkable path as a woman of the Church was not foreseen when she fell in love with the pagan Constantius.

### Mothers, sisters, and friends of the Church Fathers

Long before Nicaea I convened, and in the centuries following when more ecumenical councils were called together to

settle more conflicts in the Church, many of the most important works of theology were penned as letters, sermons, and
books. The authors of these works are honored collectively as
the Church Fathers, and the period in which they lived, the
Patristic Era, is named for them.

The Church Fathers have been highly esteemed for so
long that it is easy to forget they were flesh-and-blood men
who were close to mothers, sisters, and female friends who
supported their work and sometimes contributed to it. One
example is Saint Macrina the Younger. She was the older sister
of Saints Basil the Great and Gregory of Nyssa. Gregory, who
owed much to Macrina's theological insights, penned the *Life
of St. Macrina* to honor his sister, describing her asceticism
and scriptural knowledge.[16] Furthermore, Macrina did not
shy away from criticizing her brothers' behavior on occasion.
Gregory thanked her for the role she played in his and Basil's
paths toward holiness.

Macrina grew up in the city of Caesarea and was intended
by her father, Basil the Elder, to marry a man of his choice.
However, her fiancé died unexpectedly prior to the wedding,
and Macrina was able to devote herself, as she preferred, to a
life of prayer, study of the Scriptures, and chastity. She also
formed a community at one of her family's country homes
for women who wished to consecrate their lives to God. She
was joined there by her mother, Saint Emmelia, and women
of diverse social ranks, most of whom were virgins like her.
Intensely ascetic, Macrina refused to lie on a bed when she
was near death in her early fifties. She died on the floor on
July 19, 379.

One of the greatest Church Fathers, Augustine of Hippo,
owed much to the dogged faith and concern of his mother,

---

16 Gregory of Nyssa, *Life of St. Macrina*, ed. W. K. Lowther Clarke (London: Society for Promoting Christian Knowledge, 1916).

Saint Monica. Monica lived from around 332 to 387, primarily in Thagaste in what is today Algeria. Although she was a Christian, she was married at a young age to a pagan man named Patricius, who was an unfaithful and violent husband.

In his beautiful autobiographical work *Confessions*, Augustine wrote, "From the blood of my mother's heart, sacrifice for me was offered Thee [God] day and night by her tears." Those tears were due to Monica's long-unfulfilled desire to see her son accept Christian baptism. Describing the years he spent away from the Church while pursuing his studies and a career in rhetoric that took him to Rome and Milan, he wrote, "I have no words to express the love she had for me, and with how much more anguish she was now in spiritual travail of me than when she had borne me in the flesh."[17]

Augustine troubled his mother for years by falling into the errors of a sect called the Manichaeans and by remaining in a common law marriage with a young woman Monica deemed unsuitable for him to marry. This woman bore Augustine's son, Adeodatus, when Augustine was not yet twenty. Fourteen years later, after putting the boy's mother aside so that he might marry a young, wealthy girl of Monica's choice, Augustine underwent a conversion and determined to live an ascetic life instead of marrying anyone. This happened after he was appointed to a prestigious teaching position in Milan that connected him to the upper echelons of the Roman political and social elite—and that placed him, providentially, near Saint Ambrose of Milan, the local bishop, whose teaching was critical to Augustine's conversion.

A contemporary of Augustine's was Saint Jerome, who is also honored as a Church Father. He lived from about 347 to 420. Jerome, who famously translated the Bible from Greek

---

17  Augustine of Hippo, *Confessions*, 2nd ed., trans. F.J. Sheed (Indianapolis, IN: Hackett, 2006), 83, 85.

and Hebrew into Latin, was also a convert from paganism. From the Roman province of Dalmatia (present-day Albania and Croatia), Jerome became one of the most respected Christian priests and teachers in late imperial Rome, producing biblical commentaries as well as the Latin Vulgate Bible and influencing numerous people spiritually and intellectually.

In Rome, Jerome was close to several prominent women who lived ascetically. Among them was Saint Marcella, a widow who had devoted her life to Christian prayer, charitable service, and chastity before she and Jerome became friends. Many of Jerome's surviving letters—nearly a third of which he wrote to women—were addressed to her. Marcella and other women influenced Jerome's thinking, as he influenced theirs and offered them spiritual counsel. Indeed, after Marcella's death in 410, Jerome praised her to another friend, the virgin Principia, as an exceptional student of Scripture who was unafraid to dispute the meaning of passages with him so she might better understand them. "How much virtue and intellect, how much holiness and purity I found in her I am afraid to say ... lest I may exceed the bounds of men's belief." He added, "After my departure from Rome, if any dispute arose concerning the testimony of the Scriptures, it was to her verdict that appeal was made."[18]

Jerome's teachings inspired another Roman woman, an aristocrat named Fabiola who had divorced her husband and was living with another man, to repent publicly of her sin and devote her life to caring for the poor and the sick. In the mid-390s, during a visit to Bethlehem, she studied Scripture with Jerome. Later, she corresponded with him and influenced some of his writings.

These are just a few of the many examples of women who were important to the Church Fathers, found in the era's

---

18  Stefan Rebenich, ed., *Jerome* (London: Routledge, 2002), 125.

sources. Historical records make abundantly clear that faithful women influenced the Fathers' thinking and grounded their understanding of what Christian vocations could look like.

### The first women monastics

After Christianity had been established for several centuries as the religion of many powerful and wealthy people, not just those who were poor and obscure, some men and women sought to pursue more radical forms of Christian life than those prevalent in elite circles. Medieval monasticism—one of the most distinctive features of the Christian culture that emerged amid the Roman Empire's decline—grew out of this.

As we saw with Macrina the Younger, traditions of Christian monasticism were already in place in the fourth century. Indeed, an increasing number of Christians lived as ascetics in the Roman-Egyptian desert called the Scetes from the late third century on. Saint Anthony the Great and other Desert Fathers are the most well known, but women also retreated into the deserts of Egypt, Syria, and Palestine. According to traditional Greek sources, Saint Thaïs was one of them. She had been a beautiful and wealthy courtesan, offering sexual favors to powerful men in Alexandria, before choosing a radical new life of prayer and penance in a harsh climate.[19]

Saint Paula of Rome, as a widow, established both a monastery for men and a convent for women in Bethlehem. She was joined in monastic life by her daughter, Saint Eustochium. It is believed that Saint Syncletica, who lived from around 270 to 350, left behind a world of wealth and privilege in Alexandria to devote her resources to the poor and live ascetically, dedicated to prayer and contemplation and caring for a

---

19  Dunbar, *Dictionary of Saintly Women*, 2:242.

sister who was blind. Other women followed her. Still more are important to the early history of monasticism, including Saint Mary of Egypt, Melania the Younger, Saint Pelagia, and Sarah of the Desert.

A major development in the history of monasticism occurred in the early sixth century. This was the founding of twelve communities in the region of Rome by Saint Benedict of Nursia, who lived from 480 to around 547. Benedict famously authored a rule, or collection of guidelines, that became a standard for monasteries and convents for centuries to come.

Benedict had a twin sister, Saint Scholastica, who also founded a monastic community near Monte Cassino southeast of Rome. She influenced her brother over the years, as he influenced her. According to Saint Gregory the Great, who wrote long after they had died, the two would spend one day together each year, catching up, praying, and discussing points of theology and issues of common concern as monastic leaders. Scholastica died before her brother, and Benedict, grief-stricken, had her corpse entombed in his own monastery, where he would eventually be buried.

## Women who helped spread and defend Christianity in early medieval times

Just as women played an important part in the beginnings of Christian monasticism, they were involved in spreading Christianity and ensuring the unity and safety of the growing Church in the early medieval era. For example, a woman's pleading and patience were behind the historic conversion of the Frankish king Clovis, who founded the kingdom that would become France. Clovis accepted baptism on Christmas Day in 508, twelve years after his wife, Saint Clotilde, had first asked him to convert. Clotilde had pressed her husband for years to renounce paganism and had insisted on raising their children in the Church. Three of their sons became kings, including Childebert, who fought against the pagan Visigoths and established Christian institutions such as the monastery in Paris that grew into the great abbey of Saint-Germain-des-Prés.

Clotilde promoted the memory of an older woman she had known, Saint Genevieve. It is due considerably to Clotilde's devotion that the Church still honors Genevieve as the patron saint of Paris. Born around 420, Genevieve was inspired to become a Christian and to consecrate her virginity after hearing the preaching of several early French bishops.

Genevieve is credited with having led numerous Parisians in prayer in 451, when the fearsome Attila the Hun and his armies were terrorizing Europe. After encamping close enough to Paris that an invasion seemed imminent, Attila's armies suddenly moved elsewhere during Genevieve's vigil. When a Germanic ruler, Childeric I, was about to take Paris in 464, Genevieve famously intervened, securing supplies of grain to the city and convincing Childeric to release prisoners of war and treat her people mercifully after taking control. Childeric, as it happened, became the father of Clovis.

Early Christian queens and noblewomen also played leading roles in establishing new monastic communities. Among them was Saint Radegund, a Germanic princess from Thuringia who was forced at age ten to become the wife of the Frankish king Clotaire. Clotaire was impious, kept many women around him, and killed Radegund's brother in a power grab. Radegund fled the marriage as soon as she could, receiving safe haven in the French town of Noyon, where the local bishop made her a *diacona* ("deaconess"). Scholars debate what this meant, but it appears to have been a titular honor not having to do with ordination for liturgical functions. Rather, it was to distinguish Radegund from ordinary nuns because she was of high status and was neither a virgin nor a widow.[20]

Around 560, Radegund founded the Abbey of Sainte-Croix in Poitiers. She implemented a monastic rule that demanded strict enclosure for the women, who were expected to engage not only in prayer and contemplation, but also in reading, writing, copying manuscripts, and other intellectual and artistic tasks. Intensely ascetic, Radegund abstained from meat, fish, eggs, and alcohol. She became well known for her healing skills, which she employed while caring for the sick who came to the abbey.

Numerous other women played important roles in Europe's Christianization. Saint Erentrude, for example, was the niece of Saint Rupert of Salzburg, the bishop of Worms. Around 715, she founded Salzburg's Nonnberg Abbey, which is famous in modern times from the film *The Sound of Music* as the convent where the real Maria von Trapp was a postulant before her marriage to Baron von Trapp. It is still home to a religious community today. Another example, Saint Thecla of Kitzingen, a Benedictine abbess from England, worked with Saint Boniface in the mid-eighth century while he was the archbishop of Mainz and evangelizing German tribes before he was martyred. Long surviving Boniface, Thecla eventually governed several abbeys in German lands.

Women helped defend Christianity in some lands, including in North Africa, which by the mid-seventh century was the scene of the rapid, violent spread of a new religion: Islam. Among the rulers who labored to halt the Muslim conquests was Dihya, the queen of a Berber people in the Aurès region of what is today Algeria. Dihya led an army against the forces of the Umayyad Caliphate. She successfully held them off for

---

20  E. T. Dailey, *Radegund: The Trials and Triumphs of a Merovingian Queen* (Oxford, UK: Oxford University Press, 2023), 52–53.

a time, leading her armies to a great victory at the Battle of Meskiana. She was hailed by some people in North Africa as their ruler. But her armies were eventually defeated at Tabarka in present-day Tunisia, in one of the final stands of North African Christians against the Islamic advance.

### Irene of Athens and the Second Council of Nicaea

Not long after Dihya died, the Church in the Byzantine Empire—once known as the eastern Roman Empire—was threatened from within by divisions among Christians over the use of sacred images. This was the great Iconoclastic Controversy of the eighth century. Violence broke out between those who believed it was fitting to venerate depictions of God, His Mother, and various saints and those who believed such veneration was idolatry. The latter group, known as Iconoclasts, were able to take control of the Byzantine Empire. Between 726 and 775, two successive emperors, Leo III and Constantine V, forbade the use of icons. Christians in their domains who continued venerating sacred images were harshly persecuted.

The conflict over icons came to a head in 780 with the death of Emperor Leo IV. His widow, twenty-eight-year-old Irene of Athens, took the imperial throne in Byzantium as regent for her ten-year-old son, Emperor Constantine VI. Empress Irene favored icons and began to restore their use in churches across the empire. She also arranged for a churchman who supported icons, Tarasius, to be made the patriarch of Constantinople and called for a council of the Church that would, she hoped, settle the matter of religious imagery for good.

In 787, Irene oversaw the successful commencement and conclusion of the Second Council of Nicaea, the seventh ecumenical council of the Church and the last to be accepted by both Roman Catholics and Eastern Orthodox Christians, since the Great Schism tragically occurred in 1054. This council convened only after her earlier attempt to convene a council in Constantinople was aborted by soldiers working for the Iconoclasts, who had also tried to depose her.

Empress Irene's leadership was critical at the time of Nicaea II, and she has long been honored as a saint by Greek Orthodox Christians for this and her patronage of monasteries. She was a ruthless leader, however, who managed to rule with her son for a time but then dethroned him and reigned as *Emperor* Irene for several years. (The masculine form of her title was officially declared.) This was in 797 after she had her son arrested and blinded—as punishment for his attempt to remove her from power—with the assistance of bishops and lay nobles who were loyal to her.[21]

This remarkable woman and ruler might have altered the course of history in another way, had a project she had in mind succeeded: working out a marriage between herself and a four-times-married, recently widowed monarch in Western Europe. That prospective husband was Charlemagne, king of the Franks, who toward the end of 800 was declared to be the emperor of the Romans by Pope Leo III. Instead, her diplomatic efforts came to nothing. She was finally deposed in 802 and exiled by a group of conspirators. She died a year later. Although we cannot know how open Charlemagne was to what would have been "the marriage of the millennium", as historian Judith Herrin puts it, we might at least wonder how the increasingly tense relations between Western and Eastern Christians might have been affected had it taken place.[22]

---

21 Judith Herrin, *Ravenna: Capital of Empire, Crucible of Europe* (Princeton, NJ: Princeton University Press, 2020), 376.
22 Ibid., 377.

## Chapter 2

# The Era of Medieval Christendom

Pope Leo III's consecration of Charlemagne as emperor of the Romans on Christmas Day in 800 was an unprecedented elevation of a Western Christian ruler to a rank equal to the Eastern emperors in the line of Constantine the Great, who for centuries had guarded the Church in a special way. With this act, the pope signified that European lands that were increasingly led by Christian kings and nobles had a great leader who was called to defend the Church from her enemies.

The defense and expansion of Christian kingdoms by rulers such as Charlemagne enabled societies to emerge that, despite many differences among European peoples, increasingly shared a common culture. By the end of the ninth century, the term *Christendom* was in use and connoted all lands where Christianity was favored by rulers. Peace among all the baptized was supposed to characterize Christendom. Customs developed such as laying down weapons during Lent and embracing the chivalric code, by which Christian knights were supposed to protect people in harm's way who could not defend themselves.

The ideal was rarely achieved. As we will see, medieval saints such as Catherine of Siena and Joan of Arc knew only too well that Christendom was frequently wracked by internal conflicts. Christians often had to be called back to the heart of their faith—to repentance, fitting worship of God, the reform of corrupt institutions, and genuine concord.

From Christendom's earliest days, monastic communities especially were seedbeds of new and renewed Christian societies. They reminded the faithful, as they prospered and sometimes grew rivalrous, about what ultimately mattered: the salvation of souls and the love of God. Over time, an increasing number of these communities were founded by and for women, some of whom emerged as important leaders in the Church. Prominent among them were women appointed to the office of abbess—an office that for much of the medieval period was similar in certain respects to that of a territorial bishop.

## The great abbesses of the Middle Ages

The purpose of monastics within Christian societies was to devote their labors and long hours of prayer and contemplation to God, partly for the sake of the rest of the Church's members. It was generally believed that if some men and women were praying as full-time professionals, so to speak, other Christians could go about their ordinary business more hopefully, be it farming, making and building things, soldiery, or governing. Monastics offered their whole lives as a sacrifice, united to Christ's, to help atone for others' sins as well as their own. They helped fend off some of God's just punishments for humanity's sins. They were, in short, spiritual guardians of the Church, complementing—while giving higher meaning and purpose to—Christian rulers' and soldiers' physical defense of Christian societies.

Although monasticism emerged in the early Patristic Era, women's religious communities did not proliferate as quickly as men's in early medieval times, partly because life then was dangerous for women. In regions plagued by frequent wars among rival lords and by invaders such as the Muslim Umayyads and the Vikings from Scandinavia, there was great hesitancy about allowing women to live in communities on their own without reliable men around to protect them from rape, abduction, and slaughter by other men.

Exceptions in the early medieval period prove the general rule. Some of the great abbesses were close to Christian monarchs with armies. Saint Aurea of Paris was the first abbess of a community of some three hundred nuns who were protected by a succession of Merovingian kings, although they could not be protected from the plague when it ravaged the community in 666, killing Aurea and scores of her religious sisters. Saint Æthelthryth, Aurea's contemporary, was the daughter of the Saxon king Onna of East Anglia in eastern England and then was, by marriage, the queen of Northumbria to the north before founding and governing communities of nuns and monks at Ely.

Another Saxon princess who became a great abbess was Saint Ælfflaed, who led Whitby Abbey in Northumbria. Ælfflaed was learned, pious, and an excellent surgeon, and her community became famous for its medical knowledge and skills. Ælfflaed had been entrusted as a baby in 655 to her relative, Saint Hilda, the founding abbess at Whitby, by her father, King Oswiu of Northumbria, as an act of thanksgiving for his military defeat of the pagan king Penda of Mercia. Therefore, Ælfflaed inherited her position as abbess. Protected by her half brother, Aldfrith, who was Northumbria's king for twenty years, Ælfflaed led Whitby Abbey to some of its most illustrious days until her death in 714.

Tragically, the same abbey was destroyed by Viking invaders more than 150 years later. When a religious community finally was reestablished at the same site, it was for monks, not nuns. In the same period that Whitby Abbey was attacked by Vikings, a community of Benedictine nuns in Coldingham, Scotland, founded and led by Saint Æbbe, the daughter of King Aethelfrith of Bernicia, engaged in a gruesome act when they learned of an advancing horde of Vikings in the spring of 870. They cut off their own noses to scare away the Scandinavian pagans, who indeed were so startled by what they saw that they did not rape and slaughter the nuns. The Vikings returned another day, however. Without protection from local Christian soldiers, Æbbe and all her religious sisters perished in the second attack.

Other abbeys also suffered from invasions. The Abbey of Saint-Victor in Marseilles, home to both nuns and monks, was attacked at different times by both Vikings and Muslims, the latter of whom destroyed it in 838. The abbess, Saint Eusebia, was killed along with thirty-nine other nuns.

It was only in Christian kingdoms with strong militaries that women's religious communities began to flourish on a par with men's. By the twelfth century, numerous convents had been founded. Many followed the Rule of Saint Benedict in the wake of the great Cluniac Reform, which sought to spiritually reinvigorate monasteries across Europe that had grown lax. Some of these convents were governed by abbesses who were among the most learned people in Christendom.

Especially learned, if not saintly, was the abbess of the Paraclete in north central France who lived from around 1100 to 1163 and exercised the powers of a *praelatus nullius*—similar to a bishop in terms of her governing authority over multiple convents and dependencies. She is better known as Héloïse of Argenteuil, the tragic lover of the eminent philosopher and theologian Pierre Abélard, who had seduced her while tutoring her in the Parisian home of her uncle, a canon at Notre Dame Cathedral. She became a nun after bearing Abélard's son, Astrolabe, whom she entrusted to Abélard's sister. Abélard also dedicated himself to a religious vocation, although his vows proved easier to fulfill than Héloïse's, partly because he had been castrated by men serving Héloïse's uncle, in punishment for the Parisian love affair.

Although Abélard is better remembered than Héloïse because of his scholarship, the abbess of the Paraclete was intellectually accomplished, too. She influenced Abélard's thinking through their correspondence from their respective abbeys. Although she never fully accepted that she belonged in a convent, since she continued to love Abélard as if he were her husband despite the distance between them, she was an effective leader of the communities in her charge. She was also pioneering in her efforts to ensure that women's religious communities were tailored to women's particular struggles and gifts, not simply patterned after male templates.

### Hildegard of Bingen, foundress, mystic, reformer, composer, writer, and teacher

While the Frenchwoman Héloïse is the most infamous medieval abbess, a German contemporary of hers, Saint Hildegard of Bingen, is honored by the Church as a great mystic and teacher. Hildegard was born in 1098 in Bemersheim in the Rhineland, a region within the empire—eventually called the Holy Roman Empire—ruled by Charlemagne's successors.

Hildegard was the youngest of ten children. As was common for younger children in noble families, her parents sent her away at age eight to train for a religious vocation. A woman named Jutta of Sponheim, who lived about a half day's journey away in Disibodenberg, took Hildegard into her anchorage, or cell-like dwelling, in which she spent her days in prayer, study, and contemplation. Around 1112, when Hildegard was a teenager, a local men's Benedictine community urged Jutta to form a sister community. Within a few years, Hildegard professed vows of poverty, chastity, and obedience as a Benedictine nun.[1]

---

1    Sabina Flanagan, *Hildegard of Bingen: A Visionary Life*, 2nd ed. (London: Routledge, 1998), 2–3.

Years later, in her late thirties, Hildegard was elected as abbess. Though sometimes ill, Hildegard was energetic in her administrative and spiritual exertions. Her charisma and leadership abilities made her religious sisters and many others admire her.

A turning point came for Hildegard at age forty-two when she had a mystical experience that she described this way: "A blinding light of exceptional brilliance flowed through my entire brain. And so it kindled my whole heart and breast like a flame." Thereafter, her understanding of the Psalms, Gospels, and other biblical texts—which she had been studying since childhood—deepened profoundly. She also heard a command from God while praying: "Say and write what you see and hear."[2]

But Hildegard was afraid to obey this. All the more so because she was a woman, she knew Church authorities would scrutinize her and possibly accuse her of heresy if she wrote about divine matters. She also doubted she was equal to the task of writing about God. She fell sick as she struggled with her doubts but then became convinced that God was punishing her for disobeying Him. So she began to write a work entitled *Scivias*, part of a Latin phrase that translates as "Know the ways of the Lord."

Some clergymen learned what Hildegard was doing and indeed disapproved. But others supported it, including Heinrich I, the archbishop of Mainz, who was so impressed with *Scivias* that he urged Pope Eugene III to read it. Eugene was also impressed and encouraged Hildegard to keep writing. Eugene had been a Cistercian monk before he was pope and was a mentor of Saint Bernard of Clairvaux, an abbot and mystic who founded the crusading Knights Templar. Eugene was committed to the reform of lax clergymen and monastics

---

2    Ibid., 4.

in Christendom. He also sought the elevation of the Church's spiritual and intellectual life and saw Hildegard as helpful to these goals.

With the pope's support, Hildegard's reputation grew. She founded another community of Benedictine women close to Disibodenberg, on a hill near the town of Bingen. Based there, she exercised effective and faithful leadership inside and outside her convent. She sometimes traveled, preaching throughout the Rhineland and other parts of the Holy Roman Empire. She also corresponded over time with several popes; Bernard of Clairvaux; Eleanor of Aquitaine, who was the queen of England; Emperor Frederick Barbarossa; and other leaders. Some of these figures wrote to her after learning of her wisdom, effective teaching, and gift for spiritual counsel.

Over time, Hildegard wrote prolifically. Her teachings, drawn from her mystical visions, underscored the goodness of all of God's creation as well as the majesty of human beings because they are made in the image and likeness of God. In her *Liber Divinorum Operum* (*Book of Divine Works*), she emphasized the ability of human beings to access the divine by means of their physical senses: "Man ... rules the rest of creation, for Man is distinguished by the insignia of almighty God.... These insignia are the five human senses, through which by God's power a person understands and perceives that the Trinity in unity and the unity in Trinity ought to be worshiped in God through the right faith."[3]

Hildegard counteracted—as would Saint Dominic, the founder of the Order of Preachers, later—the heretical movement of the Cathars (also known as Albigensians). These heretics had an overly dualistic view of reality, seeing evil as a

---

3    St. Hildegard of Bingen, *The Book of Divine Works*, trans. Nathaniel M. Campbell (Washington, DC: The Catholic University of America Press, 2018), 240.

substantive rival force alongside God and His goodness, rather than as the deprivation of the good. They also associated the physical parts of creation—such as human and animal bodies and sexual acts required for reproduction—with evil. Hildegard, as a nun committed to her virginity and her religious vows, defended the physical aspects of sexuality as integral to the complementary nature of man's creation by God as male and female. She also contributed to the Church's understanding of the human person as a unity of body and soul.

In addition to writing about theological matters, Hildegard wrote about medical and other scientific topics, composed poetry and music, and directed artistic nuns in painting representations of her visions. These works of art are among the most striking that survive from medieval times.

Despite periods of poor health, Abbess Hildegard lived to the age of eighty-one. When she died on September 17, 1179, she was mourned by many people who believed she was a saint. Numerous Catholics in German lands continued to honor her as one for centuries. In our own time, Pope Benedict XVI, who had grown up in Germany and was aware of her many contributions to the Church, acknowledged her longtime informal status as a saint when he elevated her to the honors of the altar in 2012 by means of an exceptional process known as equipollent canonization. That same year he declared her a Doctor of the Church—one of only four women, so far, to be honored this way.

### Clare of Assisi, friend of Francis and foundress of a new religious order

In the High Middle Ages, Hildegard was just one of many women who contributed to a continent-wide surge in female piety and the founding of religious communities specifically for women. Among other great abbesses who did the same was Saint Clare of Assisi, the dear friend of Saint Francis of Assisi.

Clare was born on July 16, 1194, into a wealthy family in the Italian town of Assisi. Drawn to prayer and charitable works from an early age, she was ambivalent about the prospect of being married off in her teen years, as was expected of her as the eldest daughter of prominent parents, and as one increasingly admired for her exceptional beauty.

An important day for Clare occurred during Lent in 1212. She heard a sermon by a local monk named Francis who, although he was a layman, preached often in a small church called the Porziuncola just outside Assisi's walls. Francis, about twelve years older than Clare, was the son of a wealthy merchant who felt called by God to renounce all his earthly possessions and lead others to the simple, prayerful, charitable kind of life that Christ had lived. Despite much controversy, Francis had secured papal approval in 1210 for a new men's congregation, the Order of Friars Minor. Its new Primitive Rule stressed the importance of following Christ's teachings and way of living at all times.

Clare was so moved by Francis' preaching that she left home on Palm Sunday in 1212 and, inside the Porziuncola, solemnized a commitment before Francis to join his movement. She took religious vows and replaced the fine clothing and shoes she was wearing with plain garments. She also cut off her beautiful hair. This effectively was the foundation of the Second Order of Saint Francis that would in time be known as the Poor Clares.

Soon after this, Clare's father attempted to force her back home, but she stood firm—even against an uncle who tried to take her by force—protesting that the only spouse she would ever have was Christ. Adding to her father's grief, Clare's younger sister Caterina joined her as a nun, taking the name Agnes. She, too, is a canonized saint.

In 1216, Clare, Agnes, and a group of companions moved into a convent adjoining the chapel of San Damiano in Assisi. Although she was only twenty-two, Clare became the abbess of this first Poor Clare community. Her mother and another sister eventually joined her as well.

At San Damiano, Clare and her religious sisters lived in isolation, praying continuously, abstaining from meat, wearing the simplest of garments without shoes, and engaging in menial tasks such as cleaning and doing laundry. Performing menial tasks was not normal for professed nuns in this period, as most convents had a social hierarchy, with the fully professed members, who were typically of noble lineage, rarely having to labor with their hands while sisters of lower social rank did support the community in this way.

The routines of this simple life were sometimes interrupted by unexpected events, such as the unwelcome appearance in Assisi in 1224 of soldiers of the Holy Roman Empire. Clare helped to fend off their planned attack and protect her community by carrying the Blessed Sacrament in front of the soldiers and praying loudly to God. Afraid to offend God, the men dispersed.

The death of Francis in October 1226, when Clare was thirty-two, was another disruptive event, putting more responsibility on Clare's shoulders as a leader of the Franciscan movement. That movement spread and became more controversial in subsequent years, after Francis was declared a saint in Rome in the summer of 1228—the fastest anyone had ever been canonized.

One of the challenges Clare faced as an abbess over the years was to ensure that her community could follow a religious rule compatible with the Franciscan emphasis on extreme poverty and complete dependence on alms offered freely by friends. This was difficult because other communities of women inspired by Francis had sprung up and a local bishop decided to put all of them under an adapted version of Saint Benedict's rule.

Clare tried for years to free her order from this regulation but saw no resolution on the matter until just two days before her death on August 11, 1253, at age fifty-nine. At that point, Pope Innocent IV permitted the Poor Clares to follow their own rule—the Rule of Saint Clare—that forbade them from owning property and urged their members to offer penitential prayers and acts to God for the Church's spiritual reform and renewal.

Like Francis, Clare was canonized just two years after she died. Furthermore, as was true of the Franciscan friars, the Poor Clares fractured over which rule of religious life should govern them. When Clare died, the women's communities that followed the Rule of Saint Clare split from those who continued to follow the modified Benedictine rule. The former are the ones who became known officially as the Poor Clares or Primitives.

### Learned and artistic women in medieval times

Nuns such as the Poor Clares and Benedictines who were devoted to contemplative prayer were generally supposed to be drawn from the ranks of never-married virgins. The choice to remain a virgin for the sake of Christ's kingdom had been seen, since the earliest days of Christianity, as exceptionally meritorious in God's eyes. At the same time, some convents became homes to widows or even women whose husbands were still alive but who had received permission to become nuns. In such cases, the husbands typically became monks or went to fight in one of the Crusades against Muslim armies in the Holy Land, eight of which took place between 1095 and 1291.

Monasteries and convents increasingly served many purposes in Europe. They were not only centers of prayer, penitence, and the worship and contemplation of God but also
spaces in which learning and artistic activity were cultivated.
As there were fewer opportunities for women to become
scholars and artists than there were for men, convents became
important as some of the only places where women could
freely engage in literacy, study, and the arts. In addition to
supporting the Church's sacred rites though activities such as
making eucharistic wafers and embroidering vestments for the
clergy, women in convents wrote poetry, studied theology and
philosophy, and painted and sculpted sacred subjects. As was
true of Hildegard of Bingen, some composed sacred music.
Others produced illuminated manuscripts.

Although most medieval women who engaged in such work
did so anonymously, not seeking fame for it, some who were
intellectually and artistically accomplished are known to us.
A woman named Ende, probably a nun, signed her name to
the illuminations, including a stunning depiction of Christ's
Apostles, in a manuscript completed in 975 and preserved
today at the Cathedral of Saint Mary of Girona in Catalo-
nia in Spain. A nun named Guda also signed her name—and
painted a tiny self-portrait—in an illustrated collection of sermons from the late twelfth century, which is preserved at the
Staatsbibliothek in Frankfurt, Germany.[4]

One early medieval woman in a monastic community was
so dedicated to learning that she gave her life to protect a library
from a murderous pagan horde. Saint Wiborada, who lived
toward the end of the Magyar invasions of Europe in the early
tenth century, was a noblewoman from what is now Aargau in
Switzerland. She joined her brother, Hatto, at the Benedictine

---

4    Christiane Klapisch-Zuber, ed., *A History of Women in the West: Silences of the Middle Ages*
(Cambridge, MA: Belknap Press of Harvard University Press, 1992), 415.

Abbey of Saint Gall, where she learned Latin, liturgical chants, and the art of bookbinding—a skill she employed for Saint Gall's growing library. More than a century after her death, she was the first woman ever to be formally canonized by a pope, in the era when the canonization process was becoming more regularized in Rome.[5] She has long been honored, too, by Swiss Catholics, as the patron saint of libraries.

As was the case with Saint Hildegard of Bingen, some monastic women authored books in the Middle Ages. Among them was Hygeburg, an Anglo-Saxon nun in the German town of Heidenheim. She authored a biography of Saint Willibald, the bishop of Eichstätt in eighth-century Bavaria, who told her about his travels to Greece and the Holy Land. Hygeburg also wrote a biography of his brother, Saint Winebald, an abbot of the same period who participated in an ecclesiastical synod called by King Carloman I, the brother of Emperor Charlemagne.

Among the most learned medieval women was Saint Gertrude the Great, a Benedictine nun and mystic who lived in Thuringia in the Holy Roman Empire from 1256 to 1302. Mentored by an abbess named Gertrude of Hackeborn, Gertrude became steeped in the Scriptures as well as the writings of some Church Fathers and newer authorities such as Bernard of Clairvaux. After experiencing mystical visions beginning in her midtwenties, Gertrude was inspired to write. She produced many works, including her *Legatus Memorialis Abundantiae Divinae Pietatis*, which is one of the first texts to promote devotion to the Sacred Heart of Jesus. Containing spiritual exercises, it bears strong evidence of how grounded Gertrude was in the sacrifice of the Mass.

Such activities of monastic women in the realm of scholarship, writing, and the arts laid the groundwork for more

---

5   Sarah Gallick, *The Big Book of Woman Saints* (San Francisco: HarperCollins, 2007), 2.

women to pursue these activities. Among them was the Englishwoman Julian of Norwich, who lived from around 1343 to sometime after 1416. Although she is not a canonized saint, her writings have been quoted by popes, including Benedict XVI. Julian was a child in 1348 when England was hit with the Black Death—a terrible epidemic of bubonic plague that killed at least a third of Europe's population. Later in life, she chose to live as an anchoress attached to a parish in Norwich, northeast of London.

Julian wrote a lengthy manuscript called *Showings*, published long after her lifetime, that told of mystical encounters with Christ that she experienced. The work reveals that she was intimately familiar with the Latin Vulgate Bible and various classic Christian texts. And, in an era when very few women could write more than a just a few words, Julian demonstrated great skill as a writer. The poignant human tenderness of Christ's love, as well its staggering divine boundlessness, as Julian encountered it, is expressed in lines such as these, which represent a dialogue between Christ and herself in one of the visions: "Then our good Lord put a question to me: 'Are you well satisfied that I suffered for you?' I said: 'Yes, good Lord'.... Then Jesus our good Lord said: 'If you are satisfied, I am satisfied. It is a joy, a bliss, an endless delight to me that ever I suffered my Passion for you; and if I could suffer more, I should suffer more.'"[6]

Among medieval laywomen writers, the Italian-born Christine de Pizan stands out due to her range of works. Widowed young, she served as a court writer to King Charles VI of France and wrote poems, precursors of the novel, books of advice, and biographical studies. Her scholarship, which sometimes addressed sacred themes, influenced her daughter Marie, who became a Dominican nun, as well as princesses and other

---

6   Julian of Norwich, *Showings*, trans. Edmund Colledge, O.S.A., and James Walsh, S.J. (Mahwah, NJ: Paulist Press, 1978), 216.

high-ranking people. Her most famous work, *The Book of the City of Ladies*, was completed around 1405. Whereas the famous fourteenth-century Italian writer Giovanni Boccaccio, in a collection of stories about great women in history, had focused on those who were sexually immoral, Pizan highlighted examples of women leaders who were chaste, had mystical encounters, and had in some cases been willing to die for God.

## Beguines, beatas, and women tertiaries in medieval Europe

Medieval convents served social purposes too. Sometimes they offered refuge to women whose husbands were violent or whose parents tried to force them into undesired marriages. Many girls and young women were also placed in convents when good husbands could not be found for them. Indeed, convents offered food, shelter, and community to such "surplus" women, especially those from aristocratic families who were discouraged from taking on ordinary jobs, such as working as a shop assistant or farmhand, as single women of lower social ranks could.

However, because convents tended to be open mainly to noblewomen and those who could afford the communities' entrance fees, women of humbler circumstances lacked comparable institutional support when they desired to offer their lives to God in a radical way. Additionally, many women could not become nuns, despite their desire to, because they were needed to care for family members at home or in their local neighborhoods. Eventually, though, such women in some parts of Europe could consecrate their lives in other ways.

One opportunity these women had was to become a *beguine*. Beguines did not take solemn religious vows but were committed informally to celibacy, prayer, fasting, manual labor, and charitable service—sometimes in community with other women. Buildings called beguinages appeared in cities such as Leuven, in what is today Belgium, and Cologne in the Rhineland. Beguinages differed from convents in terms of the freedom the women had to come and go and not be under obedience to a superior.

Similar groups of women in Spain were known as *beatas*. Some were devoted to contemplative prayer, while others were engaged in charitable work or educating children. Groups of women like the beguines and the beatas were also found in other lands, such as the Italian city-states.

Another category of devout women in medieval Christendom were *tertiaries*, or lay affiliates of religious orders who were free to engage in charitable works outside convent walls but could still, at times, wear habits. Tertiaries also sometimes engaged in servile tasks, such as cleaning and farming, that professed religious generally did not do.

The Dominican religious family, established by Saint Dominic de Guzmán in the early thirteenth century, welcomed widows and, over time, younger, unmarried women as tertiaries. Among them was Saint Margaret of Castello, a young woman with disabilities. Born in Perugia north of Rome in 1287, Margaret suffered from blindness and curvature of the spine. As she grew up, she did not grow to a normal adult height. Her aristocratic parents were so embarrassed by this that they hid her away and eventually abandoned her at a Franciscan church in Castello when she was about sixteen. Nuns, monks, and townspeople who came to know Margaret cared for her as one of their own. In time, she began catechizing local children and caring for them while their parents were busy with work. The Dominican friars in Castello soon invited her to become a tertiary of their order. Upon her death in 1320, many people regarded her as a saint, and several centuries later she was canonized.

### Catherine of Siena and the crisis of the Avignon papacy

One of the most remarkable figures in European history was another Dominican tertiary from Italy, Saint Catherine of Siena. Catherine was one of the youngest of as many as twenty-five children of Giacomo di Benincasa, a cloth dyer in the Republic of Siena north of Rome, and his wife, Lapa di Benincasa. Born on March 25, 1347, Catherine was expected by her parents to marry at a young age, as her older sisters did, and live an ordinary life. Instead, she consecrated her virginity as a tertiary and became famous in Christendom for influencing a major event: the return of the papacy to Rome from the city of Avignon, where it had been based for seven decades while causing division within the Church.

There were signs that Catherine would not live an ordinary life from her earliest years. At around age six, she began to experience mystical encounters with Christ. By seven, she determined to make a perpetual vow of virginity and devote her life to God. Catherine engaged in extreme behaviors to achieve this, when just a few years later Giacomo and Lapa tried to push her to marry the widowed husband of an older sister who had died in childbirth. She refused to eat, cut off her hair to make herself unattractive, and held firm to the promise she made to God to remain a virgin. While upset with Catherine's stubbornness, her parents permitted her to live a life of prayer, fasting, and bodily mortifications (such as wearing a hair shirt) in their family home. She also began to help the poor and sick in the neighborhood.

A congregation of Dominican nuns lived close to the Benincasas. At age sixteen, Catherine joined them as a tertiary who was permitted to wear the order's habit. Dedicating herself to prayer, penance, and charitable service to the poor and sick, Catherine dispensed food and other necessities to the needy, praying with them and encouraging them to unite their suffering to Christ's. Some people in Siena, including clergymen, were moved by her example and began sharing their troubles with her, including their struggles with particular sins. Young as she was, she gave them spiritual counsel and developed a following. Men and women alike called her *Mamma*, seeing her as a spiritual mother. Sometimes great crowds gathered around her to listen to her talk about God.

But Catherine also had enemies because she spoke boldly about the moral laxity and corruption plaguing the Church at the time—including within the Dominican order. Many Dominicans, unsurprisingly, did not like this, and in 1374, she was called to Florence to be scrutinized by leading officials of the order.

This was providential, however, as the Dominicans assigned Catherine to a learned friar, Blessed Raymond of Capua, who became master general of the order. Raymond became her confessor and, while monitoring her words and behavior, was inspired by her joyful personality and her teachings. Despite being much older than she was, he became devoted to her like a son.[7] The two became good friends and ministered to plague victims and other sick people together.

Raymond also taught Catherine to read and write, and he documented her experiences and helped her correspond with important figures, such as Pope Gregory XI and King Charles V of France. Many of the letters Catherine sent concerned her fervent wish to see the pope return to Rome from Avignon and end the division among Christians over the papacy's long absence from the Eternal City.

In 1309, long before Catherine was born, Pope Clement V had moved the papal court to the French-protected city of Avignon in order to free the papacy from control by Italian noble families. Although Avignon was not part of France at

---

7     Thomas McDermott, O.P., *Catherine of Siena: Spiritual Development in Her Life and Teaching* (New York: Paulist Press, 2008), 46.

the time and had a feudal relationship with the Papal States, moving the papacy to a location so distant from Rome was unprecedented and caused much controversy.

The papal court was based in Avignon for several generations, resulting in several benefits to the Church: some reform of the clergy, the promotion of university education, and the consistent involvement of the College of Cardinals in electing popes. Nevertheless, the view that the popes had abandoned their true home and had become too close to France caused friction among the Christian states of Europe that sometimes turned violent. It was amid this worsening conflict that Catherine of Siena appeared unexpectedly on the scene.

By her midtwenties, Catherine had made a name for herself as an unusual Dominican tertiary who urged powerful leaders to reform the Church. Just a few years later in the mid-1370s, she was publicly criticizing the fact that the pope resided in Avignon. She also lamented that Christendom was torn apart over this instead of united around a common cause, such as going on a new Crusade in the Holy Land.

Unless they came from ruling families—which Catherine did not—women in that era generally stayed out of public affairs. Yet Catherine famously used bold language with the pope. She warned him against the evils of caring more about his own comfort and safety than about serving God properly. While the line most often attributed to her in this regard— "Be a man"—was actually written to a Dominican friar named Stefano Maconi, her letters to the pope included lines such as "Be not a timorous child, but manly" and "Be obedient to the will of God."[8]

When Gregory did not respond as she wished after sending him her first few letters, Catherine and a group of her followers traveled to Avignon to meet him in person in 1376. She

---

8    Vida D. Scudder, ed., *Saint Catherine of Siena as Seen in Her Letters* (London: J. M. Dent, 1905), 185, 235, 298.

met with him several times and offered numerous prayers for him too. One of them included these lines:

> O supreme and ineffable Godhead . . .
> Let this vicar of yours be attentive to your will, let him love
>     it and do it,
> so that we may not be lost.
> Make him a new heart,
> that he may constantly grow in grace
> and be strong in raising the standard of the most holy cross.[9]

Catherine also pressed the king of France, Charles V, to favor the pope's return to Rome, writing as boldly to him as she did to the pope.

Gregory was eventually persuaded by Catherine and left Avignon for Rome in 1377. However, he reversed his decision soon after this. After he died the following year, Catherine would go on to witness the election of two rival popes, which marked the beginning of the Western Schism—a nearly forty-year split between supporters of popes in Rome and supporters of rival claimants to the papacy in both Avignon and Pisa. This schism was still new and causing tremors throughout Christendom in 1380 when Catherine died in Rome at age thirty-three.

When she died, many people, including her mother, were convinced she was a saint. She would be canonized eventually in 1461, several decades after the Western Schism had ended.

Catherine of Siena was declared a Doctor of the Church by Pope Paul VI in 1970—one of the first two women to be honored in this way—not simply because of her influence on Church leaders in her day but even more so because of the value of her teachings and writings. In addition to numerous

---

9   Suzanne Noffke, O.P., ed. and trans., *The Prayers of Catherine of Siena* (New York: Paulist Press, 1983), 20.

letters to prominent figures, Catherine's writings include twenty-six prayers and her famous *Dialogue*. In this masterpiece of Christian spirituality, Catherine gives a lively account of the communication she received from God throughout her life.

In the *Dialogue*, Catherine put into words an especially powerful vision of Christ that had occurred early in her life. It involved the Blessed Mother, who presented Catherine to Christ. Then Christ extended to Catherine a ring and said, "I, your Creator and Savior, espouse you in the faith, which you will keep ever pure until you celebrate your eternal nuptials with me in Heaven." Thereafter, Catherine regarded herself a bride of Christ.[10] This closeness to Christ, which led her to develop an intense devotion to the Holy Eucharist, fueled her sense of mission for the Church. And it grounded the boldness with which she approached the most powerful men of the day, urging them not only to reform the Church but also to become more personally holy.

## Great queens of the Middle Ages

In addition to prominent monastics, clergymen, and exceptional figures such as Catherine of Siena, some of the medieval Church's most important leaders were laypeople in positions of authority in worldly society. Christian rulers, whether crowned as kings, queens, dukes, duchesses, or other titled members of the nobility, were understood in the days of Christendom to be specially charged by God to protect and nurture the Church in ways distinctive to them as lay leaders.

Christian queens were among those who shared, with the clergy, responsibilities of governing, growing, and disciplining

---

10   Pope Benedict XVI, *Holy Men and Women of the Middle Ages and Beyond* (San Francisco: Ignatius Press, 2012), 155–56.

the Church. An early example is Saint Adelaide, who lived during an era sometimes called the Ottonian Renaissance. Hailing from Upper Burgundy in present-day Switzerland, Adelaide was married twice, first to an Italian prince who was killed when she was nineteen and second to a Germanic king, Otto I. Wed in 951, she and Otto went on to be crowned by the pope as the rulers of the Holy Roman Empire, after Otto's armies protected Rome from the armies of another prince who had earlier attempted to force Adelaide to marry into his family. Adelaide was consecrated in a new ceremony created specifically for the position of empress, anointing her as a representative of God who stood in a line of sacred queenship going back to Queen Esther of biblical times.

Adelaide ruled officially alongside Otto and used her power to protect ecclesiastical institutions in a time of chronic warfare. When Otto died in 973, Adelaide continued to play an important role during the reign of her son, Otto II, by helping reform lax and corrupt monasteries as a friend of two saintly Benedictine abbots, Majolus and Odilo of Cluny. After her son died prematurely, she favored their ongoing Cluniac Reform in her role as empress regent for her five-year-old grandson, Otto III, and she devoted the final years of her life to charitable works and the founding and restoration of monasteries and churches throughout her domain.

A medieval queen of France named Blanche of Castile, who was the mother of Saints Louis of France and Isabelle of France, also exerted leadership in and for the Church. A member of the royal families of Portugal and England, Blanche was required in 1200 to marry the future King Louis VIII of France when they were both children. They were in their midthirties when Louis took the throne, and by then they were raising several of what would become a large brood of children. In her role as queen, Blanche influenced some of her husband's policies—for example, encouraging a royal crusade against the Cathars, as she was strongly opposed to the heresies they were spreading.

In 1226, Louis died unexpectedly. Blanche had to assume leadership over France as the queen regent since her eldest son, who later became King Louis IX, was only twelve. France was divided by warring factions of nobles at this time, so Blanche led an army to protect her son's reign. By 1229, peace was achieved under her leadership. Although further rebellions ensued, Blanche succeeded in passing the baton of power to the future Saint Louis when he was twenty, and she remained one of her son's leading advisers for almost thirty more years. Furthermore, when Louis left France in 1248 to lead a Crusade against Muslims in Egypt, Blanche took over again as regent, a role she shouldered until her death.

Well-educated, creative, and prayerful, Blanche is believed to have composed one of the most beautiful hymns to Mary of this period: "Amours ou trop tard me suis pris". She also raised all her children strictly in the Christian faith and insisted on a high level of education for them, including their study of Latin. Her daughter Isabelle became a nun who was devoted to the poor and who brought the Poor Clares to France, establishing a community in Auteuil in 1255. She was joined by the great Franciscan theologian Saint Bonaventure in this project. This is among the reasons Isabelle is honored as a saint alongside her brother and their mother.

Another prominent and pious medieval queen was Saint Elizabeth of Portugal. Elizabeth was the daughter of King Peter III of Aragon, the sister of two kings, the wife and queen-consort of King Denis of Portugal, and in time the mother of King Afonso IV of Portugal and mother-in-law of a Castilian monarch. A great-niece of Saint Elizabeth of Hungary, who was a princess devoted to charitable works, Elizabeth of Portugal became a queen in 1288 when she was seventeen. Her marriage to Denis, who was nine years her senior, proved to be a difficult one because Elizabeth was drawn to a prayerful and charitable life, assisting the sick and the poor, while Denis was much worldlier in outlook and cruel toward his wife and their two children. After fathering some illegitimate children, he forced Elizabeth to raise them.

Amid all this, Queen Elizabeth led other wealthy women to take an interest in charitable service. She also intervened to preserve peace in Portugal in 1323 when her husband and her grown son Afonso were on the brink of leading their rival armies into a civil war. When Afonso succeeded his father as king, Elizabeth was already residing in a Franciscan convent that she had established, having become a tertiary in prior years. Her reputation for holiness spread after she died in 1336. She was canonized several centuries later.

### Jadwiga of Poland, patroness of a university

Although the strong preference in medieval law was for men to inherit thrones, some medieval queens wielded power as monarchs, not just as consorts of ruling kings or regents for underage sons. Among them was Queen Jadwiga of Poland, who was born around 1373 and is honored by the Church as a saint.

Due to complicated political circumstances, Jadwiga became Poland's ruler when she was a child, and her kingdom was enlarged when she married Władysław II Jagiełło, the grand duke of Lithuania. Lithuania was still mostly pagan in the late fourteenth century and indeed was the last pagan stronghold left in Europe at the time. However, the grand duke agreed to be baptized so he could marry Jadwiga, and the royal couple supervised the Christian conversion of Lithuania thereafter.

As the Polish monarch with influence over Lithuania, Jadwiga ensured that her realm would be not only more Christian but also better educated in theology and a range of other subjects. She understood the benefits of education, as she had received an exceptional one for a layperson of the era and could speak Hungarian, Latin, German, Polish, and possibly Czech. She established a college for Lithuanians in the city of Prague, and she also provided support for a major restoration of a new but struggling university in Kraków—later renamed Jagiellonian University.

To support as many new students at the university as possible, Jadwiga donated all her jewelry to it. This enabled more than two hundred students to pursue their studies. Her hope was that the university would eventually rival the great University of Paris, where a brilliant theologian named Thomas Aquinas, already canonized by Jadwiga's time, had taught a century earlier. In time, many astute scholars, such as John Cantius and Nicolaus Copernicus, would be affiliated with Jagiellonian University, which served as the intellectual heart of Catholic Poland for centuries. Indeed, it is where a young Karol Wojtyla—the future Pope John Paul II and the same pope who canonized Jadwiga—pursued his doctoral studies in theology in the 1950s.

In her brief lifetime, Jadwiga did other things for the Church and the blossoming Christian culture in her realm. She helped establish new churches and monasteries; devoted time and resources to the poor, the elderly, and the sick; and was skilled in political negotiation, which was needed not just for her secular duties but also for her religious projects. Sadly, Jadwiga died young due to complications from a difficult childbirth in 1399. It is interesting to consider what else she might have achieved had the delivery of her child gone well and had that child, a daughter who died in infancy, survived and been raised by her.

### Ordinary women leaders of the late medieval Church

By the late medieval period, women were serving in diverse Christian leadership roles. Indeed, there are too many medieval foundresses and major patronesses of religious communities to account for in this book. But high on the list is Saint Bridget of Sweden, the daughter of wealthy landowners in Uppland, north of Stockholm. Married for twenty years to a nobleman with whom she raised many children, including Saint Catherine of Sweden, Bridget made pilgrimages to Rome and the Holy Land and then, when widowed young, founded the Order of the Most Holy Savior (the Bridgettines) for both nuns and monks. In time, she also became famous for her mystical visions of Christ. After her death in 1373 around age seventy, she passed on the leadership of the Bridgettines to her daughter Catherine, who was based at Vadstena Abbey, the order's motherhouse.

Another late medieval foundress of note is Blessed Françoise d'Amboise, a duchess from Thouars in western France, who was married for fifteen years to the powerful duke of Brittany until she was widowed at age thirty in 1457. Remarkably, this beautiful, childless widow later turned down an offer of marriage by King Louis XI of France and chose instead to become the founding patroness of the first Carmelite community in France. This was at Vannes in Brittany, where she became a nun in 1468.

While the activities of royal and noble figures are better documented, ordinary medieval Catholic women also contributed to their parishes and the broader life of the Church. Scholar Katherine French has studied, for example, ways that humble women in late medieval England—servants, seamstresses, peasants engaged in farm work—were vital to parishes. Such women worked alongside clergymen, religious, and laymen to help keep their churches clean, adorned beautifully, and well-functioning liturgically and sacramentally for the local members of Christ's Body.

The nave of parish churches, as opposed to the chancel—the area around the altar—was considered the domain of the laity, and laywomen and laymen together ensured that it was well furnished and maintained. They also "furnished the liturgy with its candles, vestments, liturgical books, altar cloths, and vessels". French observes, too, that "women's care of their parishes mirrored that of their own household," and so it was common to find in late medieval towns and villages "women cleaning, supplying, and interacting with God's house much as they would have their own".[11]

Late medieval women sometimes baked and brewed on a large scale for major feasts such as Corpus Christi, and they helped put on plays about saints to raise funds for statues and other adornments for their churches. Laywomen also occasionally served as churchwardens—parish officials charged with maintaining the quality of movable property in local churches. They helped manage parish finances. And ordinary women often donated generously to local churches—in late medieval England, typically more generously and consistently than men—in the form of bequests of jewels, furniture, livestock, and grain for the sustenance of the local clergy.[12]

Historians also know more than they used to about ordinary medieval women's devotional activities. Roisin Cossar shows that in fourteenth-century Italy—Catherine of Siena's setting—laywomen became increasingly active in terms of devotional practices and encouraged the same among others in their local communities. In the city of Bergamo, for example, some women joined confraternities such as the Misericordia Maggiore, a large charitable association. This confraternity,

11　Katherine L. French, *The Good Women of the Parish: Gender and Religion after the Black Death* (Philadelphia: University of Pennsylvania Press, 2007), 17–18, 21.
12　Ibid., 27–30, 35, 39–41.

Cossar explains, "provided women with financial security in life and prayer for their souls after death".[13]

On the rise in late-medieval Europe, confraternities were voluntary associations dedicated to penitential, devotional, and charitable activities. Women's confraternities, like men's, tended to be open to members of different social ranks and means. And their members often brought the devotional practices and deeper knowledge about Christian truths that they developed in community back into their homes, workshops, and relationships with family members, friends, and neighbors.[14]

### Joan of Arc and the medieval Inquisition

No consideration of medieval women of the Church is complete without the story of Saint Joan of Arc, who is among the most famous people in history. There is nothing ordinary about her story, although she emerged from humble circumstances.

Joan (*Jeanne* in French) was born mostly likely in 1412 in the small village of Domrémy in northeastern France. Her parents were prosperous peasants who owned their own farm. Typical of children in farming families, Joan worked at home from a young age, helping with tasks such as spinning wool and harvesting crops.

This peasant girl's ordinary days were interrupted by occasional frightening encounters with soldiers who came through the region during the Hundred Years' War, a brutal conflict between the defenders of the French kingdom and invading English armies who were assisted by French allies. As a

---

13    Roisin Cossar, *The Transformation of the Laity in Bergamo, 1265–c. 1400* (Leiden, NL: Brill, 2006), 120.

14    Ibid., 120–22.

girl, Joan witnessed an English soldier burn down the parish church of her village. At one point, she saved her father's livestock from marauders.

When Joan was in her early teens, she began hearing voices that she believed belonged to Saint Michael the Archangel and two martyrs of the early Church, Saints Margaret of Antioch and Catherine of Alexandria. The messages she received during these mystical experiences were to live a virtuous life but also do something unheard of for a peasant, let alone a young girl: visit King Charles VII of France and urge him to assert his authority. Joan thought this was strange and was afraid to obey, but she was assured by the voices that God would be with her.

The king was only about nine years older than Joan, and he had inherited his throne under trying circumstances. Members of his own family rejected his right to rule, as the royal family had members who favored unifying the crowns of England and France—one reason the Hundred Years' War raged for so long. This French disunity prevented Charles from being properly crowned after he had taken the throne in 1422. This was still the case in 1428, when Joan and a group of armed men who believed her claims about the voices traveled over three hundred miles to the city of Poitiers to try to gain an audience with the king.

Initially Joan had trouble securing a meeting with the king, which was understandable given the distrust he had toward many people in this fraught time and given, too, Joan's status as an illiterate peasant girl. Eventually, however, churchmen who examined her determined she was trustworthy. By May 1429, this strange but faithful and patriotic girl, not yet seventeen, not only had the blessing of the king of France to rally soldiers around his cause but also—in one of the most remarkable scenes in history—helped lead about four thousand soldiers in lifting the Siege of Orléans. Orléans was a city that had been brutally under siege by the English and their allies for seven months. Joan, holding up the king's colors and dressed in armor, helped lead a relief force in retaking ground around the city for the king.

During this battle, Joan was wounded with an arrow through her shoulder. But she continued to fly the king's banner. The sight of a small girl showing such courage and determination inspired countless battle-weary French soldiers to keep fighting. To the surprise of nearly everyone, Charles VII's men went on to win a striking victory at Orléans, marking a turning point in France's fortunes after many discouraging decades.

Joan was hailed as the hero of this battle and became known as the Maid of Orléans. Several months later, she was given a place of honor with her banner as the king's men won another great victory at Reims—the city in which French kings were traditionally crowned. Charles' long-delayed coronation was finally able to take place inside the city's beautiful cathedral.

Despite all this, the king began to lose his nerve as Joan urged him to try to drive the English out of Paris—the true, ancient capital of the kingdom that had been in enemy hands for a long time. In the meantime, Joan participated in more military efforts on his behalf. During one of them, early in 1431, the English captured her.

Imprisoned in Rouen, Joan was subjected to nearly five months of interrogation and humiliation by an ecclesiastical court of inquisition and prison guards under English authority. Church authorities on the English side of the war were especially troubled that she claimed that God and the saints were behind her support of Charles VII. Since she attempted to prophesy and often invoked the name of Jesus and Mary, she was suspected, too, of belonging to a sect called the Name of Jesus that was spreading at the time.

Enemies of King Charles believed that Joan was a witch. Partly because her behaviors were so unusual for a woman— and a peasant woman at that—she was suspected of all manner of sins. The fact that she wore men's clothing into battle and insisted on wearing it in prison (partly due to her fear of being raped by prison guards) was also scandalous and was the main crime for which she was prosecuted and sentenced to death as a heretic.

Joan was given many chances while in prison to express remorse and receive mercy. Her belief that she was doing the will of God was too strong, however. On May 30, 1431, she was burned to death in Rouen's market square, after having knelt and prayed for those who had brought her to this situation and asking for a crucifix to be held before her so she could focus on it while the flames engulfed her. She spoke the name of Jesus as her final word.

Unsurprisingly, Joan was seen as a wrongfully convicted saint by those who supported the French cause in the war. In Orléans, civil and ecclesiastical authorities urged commemorations of her death, seeing Joan as a God-given liberator. Within two decades, some French bishops and cardinals were speaking regularly and often of Joan as if she were a saint. And by 1456—twenty-five years after her execution and after efforts had been made to restore her name by her mother, other family members, and friends—Pope Callixtus III called a special inquisition to examine the trial records and overturned Joan's conviction.

However, many centuries passed before Joan was beatified or canonized—in 1909 and 1920, respectively. Countless French Catholics over the years, including Saint Thérèse of Lisieux in the late nineteenth century, venerated her as a saint long before this. The fact that Joan was so connected to the cause of France and had been condemned by a Church court of inquisition, even if her conviction was later overturned by

Rome, had something to do with this long delay. Joan of Arc was the first person to be declared a saint after originally being sentenced to death as a heretic by Catholic authorities.

Different from the famous Spanish Inquisition that emerged later as an arm of the Spanish monarchical state, the inquisition that Joan faced was one of many special judicial commissions sponsored by ecclesiastical and civil authorities to investigate suspected heretics in medieval Christendom. Courts of inquisition were in place by the late twelfth century and generally handed over only the most stubborn heretics to secular authorities, who would proceed with their punishment.

Although the use of inquisitions was on the decline by Joan's time, there was also a rise in claims by women about mystical experiences. Joan was just one of many to be targeted due to disagreements about whether these women were having direct encounters with God, were lying about their spiritual encounters, or were engaged in witchcraft or communication with the devil. Some scholars of the era, such as Jean Gerson of the University of Paris, who supported Joan of Arc, attempted to offer guidelines for heresy and witchcraft investigations, in the hope of stopping unfair prosecutions. Ironically, inquisitors were able to turn these guidelines against Joan and other women.[15] It would not be until the mid-seventeenth century that prosecutions like this would die down, and then only after a great increase in witch hunting victimized women far more than men in Catholic and Protestant lands, in the wake of the great fissures and disorientations of the Reformation era.

---

15   Dyan Elliott, *Proving Woman: Female Spirituality and Inquisitional Culture in the Later Middle Ages* (Princeton, NJ: Princeton University Press, 2004), 264–96.

**Chapter 3**

# The Era of the Renaissance, Reform, and Discovery

Although the late medieval period saw much discord within Christendom, it also was an era of intellectual discovery and efflorescence in the arts. Remembered as the *Renaissance period*—a phrase that connotes cultural rebirth—it was a time when some Catholics began envisioning new possibilities for their societies based on the wisdom and knowledge they drew from rediscovered classical Greek and Roman sources alongside biblical and patristic texts.

Among the possibilities envisioned was a large-scale reform of the Church's clerical hierarchy and institutional culture. By the late fifteenth century, there was growing concern that too many shepherds of the Church were morally corrupt. Some high-ranking churchmen engaged in sexual affairs and appointed illegitimate children and other family members to Church offices. Some engaged in financial misdealing. Church offices were regularly sold to the highest bidder, and many monasteries and convents were lax in enforcing their rules, partly due to wealthy patrons placing young, inexperienced family members in positions of authority. In addition, parish priests throughout Europe typically had only a basic level of education, were rarely beacons of virtue, and were sometimes minimally trained with respect to liturgical practice.

A few Catholic leaders began addressing such problems before the close of the fifteenth century. At the same time, by the 1520s, groups of zealous preachers and their followers began to leave the Church in the name of "reform", especially in German, Swiss, and French regions influenced by the new teachings of a renegade Augustinian friar in Wittenberg named Martin Luther and another heretical ex-priest in Zürich named Ulrich Zwingli. A series of movements and religious conflicts that are collectively remembered as the Protestant Reformation grew out of this. They resulted in some parts of Europe in popular uprisings against Catholic authorities and in top-down political impositions of Protestant beliefs and practices on populations that were predominantly Catholic.

As we will see, these developments proved especially hard on Catholic nuns, some of whom bravely resisted where they could. At the same time, amid the turmoil, the Church spread to parts of the world newly encountered by Europeans. In time, many Catholic women would travel from Europe to colonial territories in the Americas, Asia, and eventually parts of Africa, shaping the Church's unprecedented globalization.

None of this was foreseen, however, when a Spanish princess who would later be instrumental in connecting Christendom to other parts of the world was born in the middle of the fifteenth century, facing an uncertain future.

### Isabella of Castile, militant Catholic monarch

In the wake of the Great Schism of 1378 to 1417 that had torn Catholics apart after the Avignon papacy, and amid increasing corruption among some members of the clerical hierarchy, Catholic monarchs in Europe were increasingly emboldened to assert more control over the Church within their realms. One of the most militant and successful rulers in this regard was Isabella of Castile, the queen of Spain. Famous as the monarch who sponsored Christopher Columbus' world-changing transatlantic voyages, Isabella is also remembered for her harsh treatment of Jewish and Muslim people in Spain and for commencing the reform of corrupt Catholic institutions well before Protestant movements emerged.

Long before all this, Isabella was a young princess who was not supposed to inherit a throne. When she was born in 1451, the Iberian Peninsula was divided into five kingdoms: Portugal, Navarre, Aragon, Muslim-controlled Granada, and Castile, which was the largest of all, with access to coastlines on all sides of the peninsula. Isabella's father was King John II of Castile, and her mother was Isabella of Portugal. Isabella's half brother Henry was their father's heir, and he inherited the throne when Isabella was a toddler. However, a faction developed around Isabella when her younger brother Alfonso—the next in line to the throne—died prematurely when she was a teenager. Isabella was suddenly favored by many Castilian nobles as Henry's successor, even though her young niece, Henry's daughter Juana, had a stronger legal claim.

Isabella's position was strengthened after she married her second cousin Ferdinand, the heir to Aragon's throne. This prince, who at sixteen was a year younger than his bride, was not the original choice for Isabella. Isabella had earlier rejected her brother's plan to marry her to the much older king of Portugal. Several more failed marriage negotiations later, Isabella enraged Henry by eloping with Ferdinand and marrying him on October 19, 1469.

Although they had many enemies, and although Isabella's succession to Castile's throne in 1474 was fraught with difficulty, this young couple achieved an unprecedented union between Castile and Aragon, essentially giving birth to the modern Kingdom of Spain. This took time, however, as Ferdinand did not become the king of Aragon until 1479. Meanwhile, Isabella had to assert her authority over Castile at a time when some believed her husband should take that throne instead. To show Castile who its true ruler was, Isabella arranged that Ferdinand would not stand beside her in her succession ceremony. Even more controversially, she would hold an unsheathed sword, a highly masculine symbol.

Young Isabella proved more capable of ruling than her critics believed possible. The security of her reign was also aided by the birth of the couple's only son, Juan, along with four daughters, all of whom later became queens.

As joint rulers in Spain, Isabella and Ferdinand finished a great conquest of the Muslim kingdom of Granada between 1482 and 1492, ending any Islamic rule in Iberia after seven centuries of conflict between Christians and Moors. Also in 1492, Isabella authorized an innovative navigator from Italy named Christopher Columbus to sail across the Atlantic Ocean for the first time, with the hope of reaching Asia. The four transatlantic voyages that Columbus and his ships eventually made marked the beginning of an age of Spanish conquest, colonization, and missionary endeavors in the Americas.

Queen Isabella infamously established the Spanish Inquisition, a system of state-controlled courts designed to root out heresy throughout Spain. Initially, the Inquisition targeted Muslim converts to Catholicism who maintained Islamic beliefs and practices at home, but it soon also targeted Jewish people, who were coerced to convert and were suspected, likewise, of practicing Judaism in secret. The Inquisition's activity—which utilized intelligence gathered from neighbors, torture to extract confessions, and public punishments of the convicted—was so brutal that the pope attempted to stop some of it. But Isabella and Ferdinand ignored his directives. They also engaged in large-scale persecution of Muslim and Jewish people who refused to convert to Catholicism, ordering executions and expulsions from Spain of entire populations.

In time, the Spanish Inquisition also went after other kinds of suspected heretics, although Spain saw minimal cases of suspected Protestant beliefs and practices. One reason is that Isabella also oversaw—with the help of a talented churchman, Cardinal Francisco Jiménez de Cisneros, whom she appointed as archbishop of Toledo—an extensive reform of corrupt and lax Catholic monasteries, convents, and other institutions in Spain, as well as the establishment of a university devoted to biblical studies, the University of Alcalà. These pioneering Catholic reform efforts included the banishment of hundreds of misbehaving monks, the return of absentee bishops and parish priests to their dioceses and churches, and the production of one of the most remarkable multilingual Bible projects of all time, the Complutensian Polyglot Bible.

Isabella would not live to see many of the fruits of such reforms, as she died in the fall of 1504 at age fifty-three. By then she had suffered the loss of her son and one of her daughters, and it was decided that her daughter Juana, who was married to a Habsburg prince, would succeed her mother and father. This is how Spain, in a few years' time, ended up in the hands of a great Habsburg prince, Isabella's grandson Charles I of Spain, who became Charles V of the Holy Roman Empire. Prior to Isabella's death, another daughter, Maria, had become queen of Portugal, and the youngest, Catherine of Aragon, had married the heir to the English throne, Arthur. Arthur had tragically died young, and Catherine was awaiting her fate in England as marriage plans for his brother, the future King Henry VIII, were being debated, including the possibility of uniting him to his brother's Spanish widow.

Queen Isabella is remembered for an unusual combination of things: her ruthless treatment of Muslims and Jews; her achievement, with her husband, of unprecedented unity in the Iberian Peninsula; her devotion to her children; her own learning and patronage of scholarship and the arts; her ecclesiastical reforms; and her inauguration of Spanish-imperial expansion into the Americas. Although not a saint, she was

a formidable Catholic woman without whom important epi-
sodes in the Church's history cannot be fully understood.


## Renaissance women

As a patroness of the University of Alcalá—which became a
center of the humanistic study of ancient languages, the Bible,
and patristic writings—Isabella of Castile contributed to the
European Renaissance. The Renaissance-era flourishing of
the arts and scholarship, however, originated earlier than this
in Italy, where some of its most important patrons included
not only the famous members of the Medici family in Florence
and some popes and cardinals of the period but also powerful women. These included Isabella d'Este, who was the mar-
chioness and several-times-regent of Mantua; Lucrezia Borgia,
who was the daughter of the morally corrupt pope Alexan-
der VI; and the fierce Countess Caterina Sforza of Forlì, who
went to war with the Borgia family.

Some prominent women of the Renaissance era directed
their resources to charitable and spiritual ends. One of these
women was Saint Joan of Valois, who was the queen of France
for a time as the bride of her second cousin Louis XII, whom
her family had forced her to marry when they were children.
After her marriage was annulled by the Church, she founded
the Order of the Annunciation of the Blessed Virgin Mary in
1501 and led it as its first abbess. Her order is still active today
in Europe and Latin America.

Saint Catherine of Genoa was born into a wealthy family
in the Italian Republic of Genoa in 1447. Her father was the
viceroy of Naples. At age sixteen, Catherine married Giuliano
Adorno, a wealthy, well-traveled nobleman from one of
Genoa's ruling families. After Adorno proved to be domineer-
ing, extravagant, and faithless, Catherine, who was miserable

in the marriage, experienced mystical visions and threw herself into an intensive life of prayer, daily Mass, and service at a local hospital. Eventually her husband amended his life and followed her into a life of serving the sick and the poor. Catherine later took charge of the great Pammatone Hospital in Genoa, managing its finances and tending to patients. She also wrote manuscripts about her spiritual conversion and mystical experiences, as well as a treatise on Purgatory. These were published some years after she died.

In this period, an increasing number of Catholic women engaged in creative and intellectual work of a sort that most people then considered appropriate only for men. An accomplished poet of the Renaissance period, for example, was Vittoria Colonna, who lived from around 1492 to 1547 and came from a noble family in the region of Rome. Exceptionally well educated as a child and then married off at seventeen to a wealthy military commander of the court of the king of Naples, Colonna began to write poetry while her husband was frequently away at war.

After she was left widowed and childless at age thirty-three, Colonna moved back to Rome and resided in a convent while remaining a laywoman. There, she befriended Cardinal Pietro Bembo, a scholar and poet at the papal court who offered her his protection and encouragement. Recognizing her talents, Bembo introduced her to other poets and assisted her in publishing a book of her poems in 1538, with her name on the cover page. This was remarkable, as very few women in the period saw their work published at all, let alone under their own names. Her poems included this reflection on Christ Crucified:

> I see the Lord on the cross, stretched naked,
> with feet and hands nailed, His right side
> opened, His head crowned only with thorns,
> and on every side insulted by vile people.

He bears on His shoulders the heavy weight
of the world's sins; and in such a state
He conquers with only a heart aflame with love
both death and the furious, hostile mob.

Patience, humility, and true obedience,
with other divine virtues, were the stars
that ornamented the sun of His charity;

and thus in that bitter struggle all of these,
after His beautiful death, made brighter
the glory of His everlasting generosity.[1]

With such poetry, Colonna at times influenced her friend Michelangelo, one of the greatest artists of all time. With Colonna's poem in mind, Michelangelo drew an image of Christ on the Cross (which today is in the British Museum) and dedicated it to his friend. The two talked often about God and shared an avid interest in the ancient Greek philosopher Plato. When Colonna was eventually facing death at age fifty-four, Michelangelo visited her to help her do so with courage and faith.

Some women in the Renaissance period developed careers as artists themselves—against great odds, because talented women who wished to seriously pursue drawing, painting, and sculpting were forbidden from joining artists' guilds or formally training with master artists, even if the artists were their own fathers. All the more remarkable, then, is the story of Plautilla Nelli, a Dominican tertiary based in Florence, who lived from 1524 to 1588. In an age when all serious male artists spent long years as apprentices to masters, Nelli was self-taught. This makes the quality of her work especially

---

1    Katharina M. Wilson, ed., *Women Writers of the Renaissance and Reformation* (Athens, GA: University of Georgia Press, 1987), 41–42.

impressive. Her work was respected by her contemporary Giorgio Vasari, who published a book about great artists and said that she might have achieved greatness too had she been permitted to train as men could.[2]

Nelli's most famous surviving work is her *Last Supper*, inside Florence's Basilica of Santa Maria Novella. It is twenty-three feet long and six feet high. Nelli is the first female artist known to have painted the Last Supper. For a painting of such size, Nelli required assistants, so she taught other Dominican women how to draw and paint.[3]

Devout women made their mark in the Renaissance period as scholars too. Among them was Isotta Nogarola, who was born to a wealthy family in Verona in 1418. She and her siblings received an excellent classical education at home, as their parents hired leading scholars as their tutors. Nogarola showed exceptional promise in the study of ancient Latin and Greek texts. By eighteen, she was well known for her ability to recite eloquent Latin speeches.

Nogarola penned many works, including a biography of Saint Jerome and, more controversially, a Latin dialogue titled *De Pari aut Impari Evae atque Adae Peccato* (*Dialogues on the Equal or Unequal Sin of Adam and Eve*). The latter argued against the then commonly held prejudice that Woman is both inherently morally weaker than Man by nature, even as originally created by God in Eden, *and* more responsible than Man for Original Sin. She wrote *De Pari* while living monastically, having never married and having committed herself to prayer and solitude after receiving more hostility than praise from erudite men around her because she dared to engage them as an equal.

2    Paola Tinagli, *Women in Italian Renaissance Art: Gender, Representation, Identity* (Manchester, UK: Manchester University Press, 1997), 12–13.
3    Janice Kaplan, *The Genius of Women: From Overlooked to Changing the World* (New York: Dutton, 2020), 71–72.

## Margaret More Roper,
## daughter of the martyr Thomas More

As women began making their mark in European scholarship and the arts, some Catholic intellectual leaders began to warn their contemporaries of the dangers of educating women on a level of parity with men. The Spanish scholar Juan Luis Vives, for example, insisted in 1523 that "Woman is a weak creature and of uncertain judgment and ... should not teach, lest ... [she] drag others into her error."[4] Vives had much more confidence that men, by virtue of being men, would be less inclined to go astray from the truth as scholars and teachers, even though by then the German priest Martin Luther, the Swiss priest Ulrich Zwingli, and other learned European men were already leading souls out of the Church.

Not all Renaissance-era Catholic leaders agreed with Vives that women were intellectually less capable or reliable than men. Foremost among those who encouraged women's education was an English friend of Vives, Saint Thomas More. More was King Henry VIII's lord chancellor, who eventually was sent to his death for refusing to accept the king's divorce from Queen Catherine of Aragon. He was steeped in ancient Latin and Greek writings, as well as Christian theological texts, and he ensured that his daughters, not just his son, received the best education possible.

The most famous of More's children was his eldest, Margaret, who was born in 1505. Although she lived to be just thirty-nine, she led a remarkable life for a woman of the era, due in no small measure to the unusual degree of attention her father paid to her education.

After More began working for King Henry, he hired an excellent tutor to educate his children and encouraged them

---

4    Quoted in Theresa Ann Smith, *The Emerging Female Citizen: Gender and Enlightenment in Spain* (Berkeley: University of California Press, 2006), 24.

to converse with learned visitors to their home, such as Erasmus of Rotterdam, a celebrated Dutch scholar and writer who had produced new Latin and Greek editions of the New Testament. In this setting, Margaret and her sisters became some of the most highly educated women in Europe. They learned Latin and Greek, theology and philosophy, and ancient poetry and rhetoric—all subjects that women were generally forbidden from studying and that even most men had little opportunity to pursue.

Margaret was More's most gifted child. She wrote original Latin orations, treatises, and poems and stunned learned and powerful men, including the king, with her fluency in Latin and her facility with ancient Greek. Additionally, with her father's and Erasmus' encouragement, she published—at only nineteen—her own English translation of Erasmus' *Devout Treatise on the Our Father.*

Modern scholars of this work point to the quality of its English style—its gracefulness and straightforwardness—that makes it stand out among other works of the era. Furthermore, Margaret's translation shifted some of the emphasis of Erasmus' original Latin. For example, she subtly, with her choice of English words, placed greater stress than Erasmus himself did on the sinfulness of humanity and on mankind's need for God's mercy and kindness.[5] It seems that young Margaret was trying to help the great but sometimes too independently minded Erasmus to accord a bit more with her understanding of Catholic orthodoxy.

Excellent as Margaret's translation was, More discouraged his daughter from putting her name on the publication to protect her from public scrutiny. At the same time, he sympathized with something his daughter had to suffer as a learned woman in their culture: the constant disbelief of men who did

---

5    Merry E. Wiesner-Hanks, *Women and Gender in Early Modern Europe*, 3rd ed. (Cambridge, UK: Cambridge University Press, 2008), 153.

not acknowledge her achievements as they readily did men's. The saint once said to Margaret:

> You [are] to be pitied, because the incredulity of men ... rob[s] you of the praise you so richly deserve ... as they ... never believe, when they read what you had written, that you [have] not often availed yourself of another's help.... But, my sweetest Margaret, you are all the more deserving of praise on this account. Although you cannot hope for an adequate reward for your labor, yet nevertheless you continue to unite to your singular love of virtue the pursuit of literature and art.[6]

Sadly, Margaret's poems in Latin and Greek, her Latin odes, and a treatise she wrote entitled *The Four Last Thynges*— something More himself regarded as equal in merit to some of his own works—are lost. But her letters survive, along with her translation of Erasmus' *Devout Treatise*.

Margaret was blessed with not only an exceptional father but also a loving husband who supported her scholarly pursuits. Unlike many girls of her social rank, she was free to marry a man with whom she fell in love—William Roper, a lawyer and eventually a member of the English Parliament. William was proud of his wife's intellectual activities, and, as he had sympathies with Lutheranism, he at times engaged in friendly but spirited disagreements with his wife and father-in-law on points of Christian doctrine. He and Margaret had a happy marriage that resulted in five healthy children—four of whom were born by the time their grandfather was executed for high treason for remaining faithful to the Church.

Margaret suffered keenly when her father was imprisoned and sentenced to death by the king. Despite the shame More's execution brought upon her and her family, she and her

---

6    Thomas More, *The Essential Works of Thomas More*, ed. Gerard B. Wegemer and Stephen W. Smith (New Haven, CT: Yale University Press, 2020), 322.

husband labored to keep his papers in order and to preserve his legacy as a great scholar as well as a faithful public servant and son of the Church. Even in the face of much scrutiny by English Protestant authorities, Margaret assisted her husband in producing the first biography of Thomas More. Much of what we know today of More's virtues, family life, love of learning, and piety is thanks to Margaret's diligence, devotion, and care.

### Nuns who resisted new Protestant regimes

As the More family knew only too well, the embrace of Protestantism by some European authorities led to repressive actions against those who chose to remain faithful to the Church. Before the persecution of Catholics began in England, Protestant movements were well underway in other parts of Europe. As had been the case in the era of the Roman persecutions, many women proved to be steadfast in their fidelity as city councils and territorial governments began imposing Reformation programs that were intolerant of ancient Christian practices such as monasticism, honoring the Real Presence of Christ in the Eucharist, and asking the Blessed Virgin and other saints to intercede with God for an array of human wants and hopes.

In some German and Swiss territories, women's religious communities were either forcibly shut down or required by authorities to conform to new Protestant practices and beliefs. When convents closed, younger nuns generally were given to men in marriage—sometimes against their will. They were told that the offerings they had made to Christ of their virginity and their whole hearts were idolatrous sacrifices and a form of works righteousness. They were also instructed that obeying a husband and raising children were the only godly paths for

Christian women. Yet some religious women stayed true to the vows they had made to God despite tremendous pressure to violate them.

Protestant closures of convents meant the loss of dedicated spaces for women to pursue intellectual and artistic work, social charity, and contemplative prayer. Abbesses, mother superiors, and prioresses were deprived of Christian leadership roles that had been open for centuries to capable women who did not marry. In short, Protestant movements narrowed women's cultural, social, and spiritual options, as some modern Protestant theologians readily admit.[7]

In her book *Nails in the Wall*, historian Amy Leonard describes nuns who resisted efforts of Protestants to disband their communities or to impose Protestantism on them. In the Holy Roman Empire, for example, 50 percent of convents survived the Reformation, while only about 20 percent of monasteries did. Indeed, the resistance of nuns to Protestant impositions helped put the brakes on the attempts of political authorities to eliminate Catholicism altogether in some localities.[8]

Some convents in German territories that had embraced Luther's movement continued to take in novices despite new laws against this. Some held their ground in other ways. For example, a group of Augustinian nuns in the city of Kassel boldly told their Protestant ruler, Philip of Hesse, that they would never leave their convent. More famously, Abbess Caritas Pirckheimer and her fellow Poor Clares in Nuremberg successfully battled an all-male city council, a group of Protestant preachers guiding the city's new policies, and some of their own powerful family members to keep their convent open.[9]

---

7     Kirsi Stjerna, *Women and the Reformation* (Oxford, UK: Blackwell Publishing, 2009), 33.

8     Amy Leonard, *Nails in the Wall: Catholic Nuns in Reformation Germany* (Chicago: University of Chicago Press, 2005), 4.

9     Ibid., 5.

The Poor Clares in the city-state of Geneva were not so successful, but their resistance was especially brave. Geneva, famously, became the heart of the Swiss Reformed movement across Europe after the bishop of Geneva was exiled by republican revolutionaries and the Frenchman John Calvin agreed to lead the state-enforced reform of every aspect of Christian life and worship there. Reformation tensions had swept over Geneva before Calvin's arrival in 1536, however. In the late 1520s, Protestant preachers from the city of Bern arrived and began winning converts. Soon, violence gripped Geneva. Religious images and sacred vessels in the city's Catholic churches were destroyed by rioters. Mobs interrupted Masses and took over ecclesiastical buildings in the name of reform.

Amid all this, the Poor Clares' convent became the center of Catholic resistance. The nuns' chapel was soon the only place in the city where Genevan Catholics could attend Mass, partly because priests and monks who had been forced out of their own buildings came with weapons in hand, ready to do battle while offering Masses there. Even after the Protestants controlled most of Geneva, the Poor Clares remained faithful to the Church of the Apostles. City officials tried to get them to leave. When the women refused, Protestant men climbed the convent wall, harassing them with vulgar songs and curses. Protestant preachers also harangued the nuns with new interpretations of the Bible. Some of the nuns shouted right back, however, while others held their ears in disgust.

By 1535, the Poor Clares' situation in Geneva was unbearable. So they relocated to Catholic France, where they were able to continue their lives of devotion to God and His kingdom in peace—although as exiles from their earthly home.

Many Catholic nuns who refused to submit to the new regimes were able to flee to Catholic lands and reestablish their communities. These included English nuns who found welcome in the Spanish Netherlands (present-day Belgium).

For example, when King Henry VIII shut down Syon Abbey west of London, Bridgettine women there refused to disband and found hospitality in Flanders. The community survived for centuries but never forgot their English past. In fact, some members returned to England in 1861 when Catholics began to see reversals of their long-standing persecution in the British Isles.[10]

### The laywomen who gave their lives for the Church in England

Some of the bravest Catholic women of the Reformation era were English laywomen. Among them were Blessed Margaret Pole, Saint Margaret Clitherow, Saint Margaret Ward, and Saint Anne Line—all of whom were martyred for their fidelity to the Church.

Margaret Pole was the niece of King Richard III of England. Her uncle had lost his kingdom during the Wars of the Roses, when Henry Tudor, the father of the future King Henry VIII, took power. Marrying a cousin of the new king, Margaret survived a difficult era of dynastic transition and was made the countess of Salisbury by young Henry VIII once he was on the throne. Henry admired Margaret's wisdom and piety, so he also made her a peeress of England, with a rank equal to that of members of the House of Lords. With her wealth and status, Margaret patronized the "new learning" of the Renaissance era and was chosen to serve as the governess for the king's eldest daughter, Mary, whose mother was Queen Catherine of Aragon.

Margaret was the mother of four sons and a daughter, all of whom were adults when Henry VIII divorced Catherine and married Anne Boleyn, setting the English Reformation

---

10   Ibid., 4.

in motion. Margaret's son Reginald was made a cardinal in 1537 by Pope Paul III after opposing Henry VIII's break with Rome. He also was rumored to be involved in secretive efforts to reinstall a Catholic government, and Margaret's other sons were all arrested for their suspected involvements in Catholic plots against the king. Margaret, who also opposed the path the king had chosen, was arrested as well and spent over two years imprisoned in the Tower of London with one of her grandsons and a great-nephew. She was beheaded as a traitor on May 27, 1541, at age sixty-seven, but not before suffering the loss of two sons to the same fate.

Margaret Clitherow, Margaret Ward, and Anne Line were all arrested and executed during the reign of Henry VIII's second daughter, the Protestant queen Elizabeth I. The "crime" for which they were killed was assisting priests in ministering to persecuted Catholics. Clitherow, a young wife and mother of three who lived in the city of York, was a Protestant convert to Catholicism at a time when conversion was dangerous in England. She was arrested several times for not attending Protestant services and then risked her life by hiding Catholic priests, ensuring that Mass was offered regularly in secret for her family members and friends. After Queen Elizabeth made harboring priests a capital crime, Clitherow continued to resist the Protestant regime. She was eventually arrested and, after refusing to plead innocent or guilty, executed in York by being crushed to death on Good Friday of 1586 while she was pregnant with her fourth child.

Margaret Ward of Cheshire was an unmarried woman in her thirties when she was arrested, tortured, and hanged at Tyburn in 1588 after helping a priest escape from prison. She did not disclose his whereabouts during rounds of torture that included severe whipping with a lash. She also refused to attend a Protestant service when doing so could have saved her life. Five faithful laymen were martyred with her.

Inspired by such examples, the young Anne Line, after converting to Catholicism with her husband, harbored priests to ensure that the Mass was available to Catholics in Essex. Line was eventually caught, arrested, and hanged in 1601. Before she was killed, she reportedly said to the crowd around her scaffold, "I am sentenced to die for harbouring a catholic priest; and so far I am from repenting for having so done, that I wish, with all my soul, that where I have entertained one, I could have entertained a thousand."[11]

### The last Catholic queens in the British Isles

Among the laywomen who attempted to restore Catholicism in kingdoms where it had been overthrown were several Catholic queens, including Henry VIII's eldest child, Mary I of England, who ruled from 1553 to 1558, and Mary Stuart of Scotland, who was forced by her cousin Queen Elizabeth I to abdicate her throne and who was executed at age forty-four in 1587.

Mary I became the monarch of England after her half brother, the young and sickly King Edward VI, who was the son of Henry VIII's third of six wives, died after only six years on the throne. Loyal to the memory of her spurned mother, Catherine of Aragon, and militant in her Catholicism like her grandmother Isabella of Castile, Mary set about to restore England's traditional faith. For example, she reinstated heresy statutes, which resulted in the trial and execution of about three hundred people—among them Thomas Cranmer, who previously had led the English Reformation as the archbishop of Canterbury.

---

11   Richard Challoner, ed., *Memoirs of Missionary Priests and Other Catholics of Both Sexes That Have Suffered Death in England on Religious Accounts, from the Year 1577 to 1684*, vol. 1 (Manchester, UK: T. Haydock, 1803), 215.

Mary was cheered on by many ordinary English people who were devoutly Catholic. They welcomed the queen's restoration of altars, saint statues, and other sacred things to their original places in their churches—things that had been forcibly removed or hidden since her father's reign. But these efforts were short-lived. After Mary bore no children in her marriage to her cousin King Philip II of Spain, she had to recognize her half sister Elizabeth as her lawful successor. Mary died not long after this in 1558, at only forty-two years of age.

The red-headed twenty-five-year-old Elizabeth, as the new ruler of both England and Ireland, went on to ensure over her long reign that the Church of England and its counterpart across the Irish Sea, the Church of Ireland, would be firmly Protestant going forward. Her government forced Catholics once again to take down cherished images of saints, including images of Saint Anne, the grandmother of Jesus, and Saint Margaret of Antioch. These saints were important to Catholic women, who asked for their intercessions for good marriages and safety for mothers and infants in childbirth. When devotion to such saints was forbidden, it was traumatic for many women. Some continued to ask for saintly intercession in private, taking Catholic religiosity underground.[12]

As we have seen, English Catholic women who kept the flame of the faith alive in the Elizabethan era sometimes suffered for it. Ursula Wright of Yorkshire spent fourteen years in prison simply for teaching her granddaughter Catholic prayers and the Church's ancient liturgical language, Latin. Several of her female relatives also spent time in prison after their arrest by the earl of Huntingdon, a prominent official in Elizabeth's government.

The earl of Huntingdon was a fervent opponent of the Catholic queen of Scotland, Mary Stuart. Mary had inherited

---

12   Eamon Duffy, *The Stripping of the Altars: Traditional Religion in England, 1400–1580*, new ed. (New Haven, CT: Yale University Press, 2022), 565–93.

the Scottish throne in 1542 from her father, King James V, when she was only six days old, but she was sent away to France to be brought up there after becoming betrothed to the future French king. After she was widowed in 1560, Mary returned to her own kingdom, which at that point was divided between Catholics and Protestants and between factions of nobles. Some believed Mary should assert herself as the true queen of England, as she had a claim through her descent from Henry VII. After marrying Henry Stuart, Lord Darnley, in 1565, Mary gave birth to a son, James, who undeniably had a strong claim to the English throne should Elizabeth, still unmarried, remain childless. The matter of James' upbringing as either a Catholic or a Protestant caused more tension, as did the murder of his father—who was unfaithful to Mary and engaged in homosexual liaisons—by the earl of Bothwell, a Protestant nobleman whom Mary did not punish but instead married.

Eventually, Mary fled Scotland to escape mounting opposition to her rule. But instead of finding a safe haven with her cousin Elizabeth, she found herself under surveillance while veritably imprisoned in various castles while Elizabeth attempted to exchange military support of Mary's restoration to her throne for protection of Protestants in Scotland, which had descended into a civil war. Years later, while still in England, Mary was implicated in a plot to assassinate Elizabeth and was imprisoned and eventually executed on February 8, 1587. She wore black and crimson—the colors of martyrdom—to the chopping block and, before she was beheaded, declared in Latin, "Into thy hands, Lord, I commend my spirit."

Against his mother's wishes, young King James VI of Scotland had been raised as a Protestant. When he succeeded Elizabeth as James I of England, he secured the Protestant succession even while replacing the Tudor dynasty with the

Stuart line. His son Charles I was firmly committed to Anglicanism by the time he became king of England, Scotland, and Ireland in 1625. Nevertheless, Charles married a staunchly Catholic princess, Henrietta Maria of France, the sister of King Louis XIII. Henrietta Maria had been formed by her mother, Queen Marie de' Medici, to be fervent in her faith, and her becoming queen of England—and her mere presence in England, especially once she had borne an heir whose faith she sought to influence—caused great tension.

As queen, Henrietta Maria advocated for Catholics and attempted to restore Catholic worship in England. Her activities, though, fueled radical Protestant opposition to her husband's rule in the English Parliament, which was increasingly in the thrall of the Puritan leader Oliver Cromwell. Cromwell took over England as a dictator after Charles I was executed. Henrietta Maria, exiled in France at the time of Charles' beheading, was so stunned by the news that she could not move for several hours after receiving it. She spent her last years founding convents in France and unsuccessfully attempting to convince the French Crown to back an armed restoration of Catholicism in England.

### Women and the early Jesuits

Among the families in Elizabethan England who practiced Catholicism in secret were the Wards of Mulwith in Yorkshire. A baby girl named Joan—the granddaughter of the aforementioned Ursula Wright—was born to this family in 1585. She grew up admiring priests of the Jesuit order who were daring in ensuring that English Catholics received the sacraments and were instructed in the full Christian faith. Formed in 1534 in Paris by Saint Ignatius of Loyola from Spain and six of his friends, the Society of Jesus by Joan's time was one of the most successful religious orders in the Church's history, with schools, missions, and other ministries across Europe, the Americas, Africa, and Asia. By the time Joan was born, five Jesuits had been martyred for their fidelity to the Catholic faith in England; in time that number would climb to twenty-eight. Famous among them was Saint Edmund Campion, who had been boldly public in his witness and had been hanged, drawn, and quartered at Tyburn in 1581.

Growing up with such stories of Catholic heroism, young Joan Ward—who became known by her confirmation name Mary—decided to pursue a religious vocation at a time when English Catholic girls could do so only by leaving their homeland. Father Richard Holtby, her Jesuit confessor, helped convince her family to accept the plan, despite their hopes that she would marry. At age twenty-one, Mary Ward left England for a convent of Poor Clares in Saint-Omer, a Spanish-controlled city that is today in northern France. With the dowry she brought with her, she was soon able to found a new community of Poor Clares at Gravelines that other Englishwomen were invited to join.

Ward grew restless, however, because she desired to pursue an active ministry, such as the education of girls, rather than live according to the rule of the contemplative order she had joined. In 1609, she and some companions established a new congregation and started several schools for girls. Ward had in mind a model of religious life for women patterned after the Jesuits'. This, however, ran counter to the Church's insistence on a strictly cloistered life for nuns, which had been its position since 1563 as a result of the Council of Trent's reforms. Calling her congregation the Sisters of Loreto, Ward crisscrossed Europe, establishing schools for girls that were similar to the Jesuits' colleges for boys. These schools cropped up in the Spanish Netherlands, German and Austrian territories, Italy, and France.

Over time, the Sisters of Loreto enjoyed the support of powerful Catholic monarchs, including Holy Roman Emperor Ferdinand II, Elector Maximilian I of Bavaria, and Archduchess Isabella Clara Eugenia, who ruled the Spanish Netherlands. They also had the support of several prominent Jesuits and leading churchmen.

However, Ward and the Sisters of Loreto were mocked by others as "galloping girls" and "Lady Jesuits". Jesuits themselves were divided about the women: some were concerned that they were trying to become a female branch of the Society, something forbidden in the Jesuits' Constitutions. In 1631, the Jesuit superior general, Mutio Vitelleschi, secured a temporary suppression of the Sisters of Loreto from Pope Urban VIII. Urban's decree referred to Ward's "Jesuitesses" as a "sect" whose apostolic activities, such as catechizing and helping poor and young girls outside cloister walls, was unsuited to "the weakness of [the female] sex, intellect, womanly modesty and above all virginal purity".[13]

Despite this, Ward was able to establish a new community in her home country—the same country she had once had to flee to become a nun—because the Catholic queen Henrietta Maria was at that time influencing matters, prior to Cromwell's Puritan dictatorship. Furthermore, the Sisters of Loreto were eventually given full approval by a later pope, Benedict XIV, but that recognition did not come until 1749, long after their foundress had died in 1645. Ward's order would eventually spread throughout the world, including to India. Indeed, Saint Teresa of Calcutta, to whom we will turn later in the book, started out as a Sister of Loreto before forming the Missionaries of Charity.

---

13   Laurence Lux-Sterritt, "Mary Ward's English Institute and Prescribed Female Roles in the Early Modern Church", *Gender, Catholicism and Spirituality: Women and the Roman Catholic Church in Britain and Europe, 1200–1900*, ed. Laurence Lux-Sterritt and Carmen M. Mangion (London: Palgrave Macmillan, 2010), 94.

Unsurprisingly, Mary Ward's conflicted relationship with the Jesuits has fascinated scholars. And admirers of Ward to this day do not understand why the Jesuits were and remain so strongly opposed to having a women's branch as so many other orders, such as the Benedictines and Dominicans, do.

Little known, however, is that Ignatius of Loyola was initially required by Pope Paul III to welcome women as Jesuits in the founding era. This was due to the influence of his close friend and aristocratic patroness Isabel Roser, a young widow who had earlier sponsored his education at the University of Paris, where he met the men who would become the first Jesuits. Roser's connections in Rome, in fact, facilitated Loyola's efforts to meet with the pope in the first place to receive approval of his order.

Roser's influence was such that the pope allowed her and two of her friends to become the first female members of the Society of Jesus—against Loyola's wishes. The women professed vows on Christmas Day in 1543. In the meantime, Roser had gifted most of her estate to the Jesuits, which was critical to sustaining early Jesuit ministries, such as the Casa Santa Marta, a home for repentant prostitutes. Unfortunately, Roser and Loyola stopped getting along. They began to squabble about financial matters, and Loyola did not want his priests bound to convents as spiritual directors. Upon Loyola's orders, Roser and her religious sisters left the Society by late 1546, returning to Spain and pursuing prayerful and charitable vocations there. Loyola subsequently got the pope to agree that women living in community would never again be entrusted formally to Jesuits.[14]

Regardless, Roser's patronage and the influence and support of other women in Loyola's life were critical to the

---

14  Jean Lacouture, *Jesuits: A Multibiography*, trans. Jeremy Leggatt (Berkeley, CA: Counterpoint, 1997), 141, 151–54.

formation and early success of the Jesuits. Loyola's sister-in-law, Magdalena de Araoz de Loyola, had urged him to read a book of saints' lives and the monumental *Life of Jesus Christ* by Ludolph of Saxony when, as a young man, he was recovering from a battle wound at his family's castle. These books changed his life and set him on the path that eventually led to his true calling. Furthermore, during his "pilgrim" years of traveling throughout Spain and developing his *Spiritual Exercises* as a layman, Loyola was aided in his unusual work (which attracted the notice of the Inquisition) by an array of aristocratic women.

Women wielded considerable influence on the Society of Jesus as it developed dramatically and quickly, with schools, missions, and other ministries multiplying throughout Europe and around the world. Among these women was Princess Juana of Austria, who was the daughter of Holy Roman Emperor Charles V. When she was quite young, she was also the temporary ruler of Spain on behalf of her brother, King Philip II, while he was in England as the husband and consort of Queen Mary I.

In 1554, Loyola allowed Juana to enter the Jesuit order secretly under the pseudonym Mateo Sánchez and to train as a scholastic, or vowed member of the order educated according to the Society's rigorous norms. Publicly this was unknown, however, as the princess employed her position in Spain to protect the Jesuits during a period when they faced great opposition from political and ecclesiastical officials in her country. In the years after Loyola's death, the Jesuits, with Juana's assistance, finally were favored by the Crown of Spain and started serving as missionaries in Spanish colonies abroad.[15]

---

15  Hugo Rahner, S.J., ed., *Saint Ignatius Loyola: Letters to Women*, trans. Kathleen Pond and S.A.H. Weetman (New York: Herder & Herder, 1960), 59; James W. Reites, "Ignatius and Ministry with Women", *The Way* 74 (1992): 15–16.

The early Jesuits owed a great deal, too, to a Portuguese noblewoman, Doña María de Guadalupe de Lencastre y Cárdenas Manrique, who eventually became the duchess of Aveiro. In the late seventeenth and early eighteenth centuries, she was a major patroness of the Society's missions in Africa, Asia, and the Pacific region. In this, she was one of many women with whom the Jesuits collaborated in the development of their storied missions across the globe.

In early modern Japan, for example, where one of the first Jesuits, Saint Francis Xavier, established a mission in 1549, female catechists were critical to the Jesuits' early evangelization efforts. Japanese women who embraced Catholicism sometimes preached and, according to historian Haruko Nawata Ward, "disputed with Buddhist priests, translated and wrote Christian literature, persuaded and helped women and men convert to Christianity", and baptized converts when priests could not be present.[16]

The young Japanese church faced a great deal of persecution, however. Some Japanese women who helped spread the faith suffered greatly. Among them was Blessed Hayashida Magdalena from Kitaarima near Nagasaki, who had consecrated her virginity and was later burned alive by a Japanese warlord in 1613. Only eighteen, she was martyred alongside her parents and young brother.

In the Jesuits' early mission to China, indigenous women supported the priests as patronesses and helped communicate Christian messages in domestic spaces that the missionaries could not enter because of strict gender divisions in Chinese society. Indeed, the early history of the Church in China cannot be understood without reference to such collaborations among Jesuit priests and local women—as well as local

---

16  Haruko Nawata Ward, "Jesuits, Too: Jesuits, Women Catechists, and Jezebels in Christian-Century Japan", in *The Jesuits II: Cultures, Sciences, and the Arts, 1540–1773*, ed. John W. O'Malley et al. (Toronto: University of Toronto Press, 2006), 640, 643.

men, it should be underscored, who in some cases became Jesuits themselves.[17]

In French colonial North America, where Jesuits such as Saint Isaac Jogues and Saint Jean de Brébeuf were martyred in the 1640s, the priests of the Society depended on local Native American and French people, many of them women, for the success of their mission. Sometimes native women and men taught Christian doctrines to prospective converts to the Church in their home villages or family networks. They also helped lead the prayer life of mission communities when the Jesuits could not be present. And sometimes they ran schools attended by native and French children alike.

The most famous Native American of this context, who was also devoted to charitable service along with other native women she knew, is Saint Kateri Tekakwitha, whom we will encounter later in this chapter. We will also see that there were important consecrated French women who worked with the Jesuits in French North America and were some of the first female missionaries ever to be sent overseas for the Church.

Back in Europe, despite the rocky road in the time of Ignatius of Loyola and Isabel Roser, the early Jesuits had fruitful relationships with religious women—such as Saint Teresa of Avila and Saint Margaret Mary Alacoque—that deeply marked the Church's life. As we will now see, these relationships played out very differently from what happened with Mary Ward.

### Teresa of Avila, great reformer of Catholic religious life

In a time of growing unrest over the divisions caused by the Protestant movements, the Jesuit order from its beginnings

---

17 Nadine Amsler, *Jesuits and Matriarchs: Domestic Worship in Early Modern China* (Seattle: University of Washington Press, 2018).

became synonymous in Europe with Catholic efforts to reform and renew the Church. In addition to the Jesuits, other religious congregations established in the early modern period contributed to the Church in related ways, such as the Company of Saint Ursula (known as the Ursulines) formed by Saint Angela Merici in Italy in 1535. The Ursulines, who were devoted to the education of girls, sometimes worked closely with Jesuits, including in mission settings.

Also famous from the period—but focused differently on the renewal of cloistered, contemplative religious life in the wake of Protestant attacks on monasticism—were the Discalced Carmelites established by Teresa of Avila in Spain in 1579. Teresa, who has been honored as a Doctor of the Church since 1970, was a Spanish nun remembered for her mystical visions of Christ and her tireless efforts to reform the Carmelite order, which had grown lax since medieval times. And although Teresa never encountered any Protestants, since Spain saw few inroads by them, she has long been regarded as one of the great reformers and spiritual leaders of what has traditionally been called the Counter-Reformation but is referred to as the Catholic Reformation by historians today.

Similar to Loyola, Teresa did not discern her primary mission for God and the Church until she was middle-aged, after she had experienced an awakening in her faith at age thirty-nine.

Teresa was born on March 28, 1515, in the fortified city of Avila in central Spain. Her full name, Teresa Sánchez de Cepeda y Ahumada, signaled that her family was a noble one. But there was a whiff of scandal around her father Alonso's side of the family, as it included Jewish ancestors who had been forced to convert to Catholicism in the wake of Queen Isabella of Castile's repressive measures. Teresa's grandfather was even condemned by the Inquisition for practicing Judaism in secret. He recovered his reputation as a Catholic, however, and when Teresa was growing up, her family encouraged Catholic piety.

Teresa, who was one of eleven children, had a quiet childhood in Avila. Her mother, Béatriz, encouraged her education but also her reading of romances—something Alonso did not approve of. Teresa was close to a brother with whom she attempted to run away so they could die as martyrs in a Muslim land: a sixteenth-century Spanish-Catholic version of children's imaginations running wild. The happiness of her childhood ended, however, when Teresa was thirteen and her mother died. Within two years, Teresa's own health deteriorated.

During a difficult period when she was bedridden, Teresa developed a love for prayer. When she recovered her health, however, she became absorbed in the typical interests of wealthy teenage girls. She was pretty, loved fine dresses in bright colors, and was preoccupied with dreams of falling in love. And yet— partly because it was simply something that many intelligent girls from aristocratic families did—she entered a convent in her hometown. She was twenty when she became a Carmelite, and she did so against her father's wishes.

In the convent, Teresa was serious about some aspects of her religious life. As was the case with too many monastic institutions in that period, however, the culture of the convent was worldly, as the strict Carmelite rule had been loosened and ignored over time. Guests came and went freely, despite the formal rule of strict enclosure behind cloister walls, and for years Teresa was often left to her own devices, both spiritually and morally.

Almost two decades after she became a nun, Teresa underwent a profound interior conversion. After looking at a powerful image of the wounded Christ, she began to have mystical experiences that she later described as moments of perfect union with God in which she gained clear insights into divine mysteries. In this period of her mystical awakening, she was also frequently given the "blessing of tears" and came to understand the nature of sin and the terror of Hell as alienation from God.

Some of Teresa's friends feared she was under demonic influences. But her confessor, the Jesuit Saint Francis Borgia, was convinced that God was communicating with her in a special way and calling her to a special mission. By 1558, encouraged by Borgia and another Jesuit, Juan de Prádanos, who taught her about spiritual discernment, Teresa was experiencing powerful visions of Christ in which He appeared to her in bodily form and had lengthy conversations with her. Teresa would undergo ecstatic states during these visions, which embarrassed her whenever it happened in the presence of other nuns.

Prompted by Christ's messages in her visions, Teresa became full of zeal to return the Carmelite order to its original apostolic way of life. This was five years before the Council of Trent would issue its final decrees, including important ones concerning the reform of religious life throughout the Catholic world.

Many of the 150 women in Teresa's community were inspired by the mystic's zeal and joined her when she left her convent to establish a new one dedicated to reform, the Convent of San José. There, she was able to lead her sisters in living radical poverty and following a strict regimen of prayers, devotions, and contemplation of the divine mysteries. Teresa wished to return all Carmelites, female and male, to their original rule. Carmelite nuns and monks, as she understood it, were to live in a manner radically dedicated to God and to penance—indeed, to live a vocation of reparation for the sins of mankind, including the sins of priests who were often mired in worldliness.

Although Teresa had permission from Pope Pius IV to open her new convent, Catholic leaders in and around Avila opposed what she was doing. In the coming years, Teresa's reform efforts would be fought by powerful people in the Church in Spain, including leading Carmelites. However, she was supported in her work by the order's prior general in Rome, and she was emboldened to establish more reformed Carmelite communities throughout Spain, including some monasteries for men. She was aided in the latter project by a new friend, a young monk whom she mentored named Juan de Yepes—later known as Saint John of the Cross. In 1568, under Teresa's influence, John opened the first reformed Carmelite monastery in Duruelo, north of Madrid.

Teresa worked tirelessly to establish reformed Carmelite communities despite frail health as she aged and despite the forceful opposition of many authorities. One such dispute played out in 1575 in the city of Seville when some reformed Carmelite friars disputed with friars of the established Carmelite order. Teresa attempted to quiet this dispute, but the Carmelites' superior general ordered her to return to her convent and stop founding new communities.

Teresa had some powerful friends, however, including King Philip II, who admired her. With his intervention, the reformed branch of the Carmelites was given independent jurisdiction in Spanish realms in 1579—something Pope Gregory XIII confirmed in 1580. Teresa thus was able to continue with her reform until her last days, and the branch of the Carmelites she founded became known as the Discalced Carmelites. *Discalced* alludes to the fact that the nuns and monks wore simple sandals, without stockings or socks.

In addition to her mystical experiences and success as a reformer, Teresa was beloved by many of her fellow religious—and many priests too—for her gifts as a spiritual director. She is also famous for her writings on spiritual matters. However, Teresa was reluctant to write about her experiences or spiritual insights because she knew she could get in trouble with the Inquisition. Women, especially, were scrutinized when they commented on divine matters, and even more so when they claimed to have direct contact with God.[18]

But Teresa's spiritual directors urged her to write. In time, the works she produced on monastic asceticism and the contemplative vocation would establish Teresa as one of the greatest spiritual masters of all time. By the end of her life, Teresa had written an abundance of material, not just for a woman of her time but also for a leader of other religious who was busy with the founding and administration of many institutions. Her autobiography was eventually published in 1611, some years after she died. She also wrote a chronicle of her work in founding Discalced Carmelite communities. That book, the *Book of the Foundations*, was published in 1610. Her other writings include *The Way of Perfection*, which was released in 1583, and *The Interior Castle* and *Exclamations of the Soul to God*, which were published five years later. She also wrote poems and letters to many people.

In her final years, Teresa suffered poor health and more opposition from local Church authorities who attempted to restrict her influence. This is one reason her works were not published until after her death on October 15, 1582, when she was sixty-seven. She died in the company of her religious sisters, and her last words included lines from the Song of Songs as well as an exclamation to Christ that the hour she had been longing for, of finally joining her divine spouse in unending union, had finally come.

Despite the controversy surrounding her in Spain, Teresa of Avila was canonized relatively quickly. Pope Gregory XV raised her to the honors of the altar in 1622, the same year Ignatius of Loyola was canonized. Eventually she was made

---

18  Carlos Eire, *The Life of Saint Teresa of Avila: A Biography* (Princeton, NJ: Princeton University Press, 2019), 42, 108–10.

a patron saint of Spain. Furthermore, in the seventeenth century, the Discalced Carmelites spread to other countries and flourished as an order. For example, Discalced Carmelites exerted much influence on the reform of the Church in France, just as they were doing in Spain.

For centuries, Catholics all over the world have drawn nourishment from Teresa's spiritual wisdom. In *The Interior Castle*, for example, she warns Christians against the subtle temptations that come with progress in the spiritual life, such as pride, excessive zeal, sentimentalism, and the desire of being acknowledged by others as a saint. She advises that successful struggles against such things come only with God's help. At the same time, she counsels that being scrupulous about one's own responses to these temptations can lead to either despair or narcissism.[19] The goal, then, is always to stay focused on God, not oneself, and to move forward confidently with the help of the sacraments of the Church and with *courage*, a virtue that Teresa believed women could exercise as much as men could and one that she modeled often in her remarkable life.

### Margaret Mary Alacoque and the spreading devotion to the Sacred Heart

Margaret Mary Alacoque's story is less well known than Teresa of Avila's, yet the impact of Alacoque on the spiritual life of the Church is immeasurable. Alacoque, along with some clergymen she knew, played a critical role in spreading devotion to the Sacred Heart of Jesus beyond a few isolated places in the Church of her time, but only after she had reported to her mother superior that she had experienced mystical visions concerning the Sacred Heart and hardly anyone believed her.

---

19  Wilson, *Women Writers of the Renaissance and Reformation*, 409.

Fortunately, one Jesuit, Saint Claude de La Colombière, did, and his support was integral to the devotion's eventually being promoted by the universal Church.

Alacoque was born on July 22, 1647, in Burgundy in eastern France. Drawn since childhood to intensive hours of prayer before the Blessed Sacrament, she eventually at age twenty-four joined the Order of the Visitation, founded by Saints Francis de Sales and Jane de Chantal, despite her mother's encouragement to find a husband. She took solemn religious vows at the Convent of Paray-le-Monial in Burgundy in late 1672.

About a year later, Alacoque experienced the first of several visions relating to the Sacred Heart. In her visions, she received instructions from Christ and the Blessed Mother to promote devotion to the Sacred Heart by means of regular reception of Communion on the first Friday of every month, eucharistic holy hours on Thursdays, and wider celebration of a new liturgical feast day, the Feast of the Sacred Heart. The latter had been honored in the French diocese of Rennes since 1670, thanks to the efforts of Saint John Eudes and a local bishop. In the first of Alacoque's visions, Christ invited her to rest her head upon His breast, revealed marvelous truths about the boundless depths of His love, and encouraged her to tell others about His messages to her.

Devotion to the Sacred Heart of Jesus was not new in Alacoque's time. It had grown out of a long tradition of devotions to Christ's five wounds with foundations in the writings of the Church Fathers and support from medieval popes and synods. Medieval saints such as Anselm of Canterbury and Gertrude the Great had promoted early forms of the devotion.[20] By the time Alacoque was growing up, some theologians

---

20    Joseph J.C. Petrovits, *Devotion to the Sacred Heart: Its Theology, History and Philosophy* (St. Louis: B. Herder, 1918), 14–15.

and preachers, including Jesuits, were promoting devotion to the Sacred Heart among the faithful. And Alacoque's own Visitation order, founded in the seventeenth century, had taken for its coat of arms an image of Christ's Heart, with a cross at the top, that was pierced with two arrows and encircled by the Crown of Thorns.[21]

Yet Alacoque found little receptivity inside her convent to her messages from Christ. Nor did she find much receptivity among theologians and Church officials who looked into her case. However, the independent-minded Father Colombière, the newly assigned Jesuit confessor to her community, believed her. In time, he convinced others and began spreading devotion to the Sacred Heart in line with Alacoque's visions. Eventually, a new mother superior at Paray-le-Monial also championed Alacoque's visions and the devotion.

After Colombière died at age forty-one in 1682 and Alacoque followed him in 1690 at age forty-three, the Jesuits promoted the Sacred Heart devotion energetically. In the following century, beginning in 1765 with Gregory XVI, popes began to encourage the celebration of the Mass of the Sacred Heart. By 1856, the Feast of the Sacred Heart was added to the Roman calendar, for celebration by the universal Church every year. Veneration of Alacoque and Colombière also spread. The two were canonized in 1920 and 1992 respectively.

### Louise de Marillac, foundress of a new kind of congregation for the poor

On March 15, 1660, when Margaret Mary Alacoque was still a child, a consecrated Frenchwoman whose life and work would prove to be of tremendous consequence to the Church died in

---

21   Ibid., 18.

Paris. This was Saint Louise de Marillac, who cofounded, with Saint Vincent de Paul, the secular congregation for women that became known as the Daughters of Charity. In time, due to their combination of contemplative prayer and care for the poor, sick, and marginalized, the Daughters would become one of the most successful Catholic congregations in the world. Furthermore, they would change perceptions of what women's consecrated life could look like.

De Marillac's story is tied not only to de Paul's but also to those of many devout Catholics during a period that was a golden age for the Church in France. There are many great names associated with it, including Francis de Sales, Jane de Chantal, and John Eudes, who have already been mentioned; Pierre de Bérulle, the founder of the French Oratory and the progenitor of the French school of spirituality; Mother Madeleine de Saint-Joseph, a Discalced Carmelite whose cause for sainthood has been open in Rome for over three centuries; Jean-Jacques Olier, the founder of the Society of Saint Sulpice for clergymen; Blaise Pascal, the brilliant mathematician and author of the *Pensées* who tried to reach a rising generation of religious skeptics with Christianity's core teachings; and Bishop Jacques-Bénigne Bossuet, Louis XIV's eloquent court preacher whose *Discourse on Universal History* became a theological and philosophical classic.

De Paul himself, who in the 1610s rose up from an obscure peasant background to become a well-known priest in elite French circles, became famous as the founder of the Congregation of the Mission, a society of apostolic life for men devoted to the clergy's spiritual renewal and to providing religious instruction, the sacraments, and alms to the poor. By the mid-1620s, he was also collaborating with a network of laywomen who were dedicated to charitable service and who became known as the Ladies of Charity. Still active today, the Ladies are the oldest Catholic laywomen's organization in the world.

De Paul was just a ten-year-old boy in southern France—and the kingdom was in the final throes of devastating wars between Catholics and Protestants—when Louise de Marillac was born in 1591 in Le Meux, north of Paris. Although of noble ancestry, she was the product of an illicit affair between her prominent aristocratic father, Louis de Marillac, and a woman whose identity is lost to history.

Louise's father was unable to persuade his wife to accept his illegitimate daughter, so Louise was sent as a small child to a Dominican convent in a town called Poissy, where she was raised by the nuns. Her father died when she was a young teenager, still living with the nuns. Her uncle, Michel de Marillac, who eventually became a leading royal councillor, stepped in to serve as her legal guardian.

Receiving from the Dominicans an excellent education for a girl of that time, Louise also developed a serious prayer life and a strong devotion to the Mass. Hoping to become a nun herself, she applied at age fifteen for admittance into a new religious congregation, the Daughters of the Passion, who were affiliated with the Capuchins. However, she was turned down. Her powerful relatives wished for her to marry anyway. Not long after this, she married a royal secretary, Antoine Le Gras, who was fourteen years her senior. They had a son, Michel, when Louise was twenty-two.

Ten years later, in 1623, Antoine fell ill. Although he would live another two years, Louise sensed that her husband did not have much time left, and this sent her into a spiral of scrupulosity about a desire she had been unable to suppress during her married life: to become a cloistered nun. This longing strengthened as her husband's health declined, and she felt guilty about it.

A key moment for Louise came on Pentecost Sunday in 1623. She experienced in prayer a most profound consolation from God, assuring her that she would, indeed, be able to devote herself radically to Him soon. She wrote these words about the experience: "My mind was instantly freed of all doubt. I was advised that I should remain with my husband and that a time would come when I would be in a position to make vows of poverty, chastity, and obedience and that I would be in a small community where others would do the same.... I felt that it was God who was teaching me these things."[22]

Around the time that Louise became a widow, in 1625, she met Vincent de Paul. Neither had any idea then how interwoven their lives would become. Indeed, Louise was not drawn to Vincent initially. Eventually, however, she began taking spiritual direction from him, after he recognized that she often fell prey to self-criticism and might find peace and joy if she trusted more in God's Providence and merciful love.

This was the beginning of a lifelong friendship in which the strengths of both Louise and Vincent would rub off on each other over the years—at times with some very human friction. Vincent was warm by nature and in tune with the ways God's love spoke to the heart. He also liked to wait cautiously rather than to act quickly on matters related to his work and the spiritual progress of his friends and associates. Louise, for her part, was by nature highly rational and experimental. She often wanted to try out—more quickly than Vincent recommended—different prayer regimens and ways of practicing the Christian life.

The great fruit of this relationship was the Daughters of Charity, which emerged from Louise's work with the Ladies of Charity. Over time, Louise and Vincent noted that the Ladies' assistance to the poor suffered from dwindling numbers. And, especially in more urban settings, the aristocratic women involved were discouraged by social custom from working

---

22 Frances Ryan, D.C., and John E. Rybolt, C.M., eds., *Vincent de Paul and Louise de Marillac: Rules, Conferences, and Writings* (New York: Paulist Press, 1995), 226–27.

too closely with poor, sick, and marginalized people. The two future saints realized that a new organization was needed: one made up of women from humbler backgrounds who were free to engage full time in charitable service. De Marillac elected to lead this new organization, welcoming a group of such women into her Parisian home and training them.

The Daughters of Charity, founded in 1633, grew quickly. By the end of Louise and Vincent's lives in 1660 (the two died just a few months apart), the Daughters had grown from a small group to more than eight hundred women who worked in many places throughout France. But this was not at all a foregone conclusion, given the roadblocks the Daughters faced when seeking recognition from ecclesiastical and political authorities.

The main problem was that, with their gray dresses and white turbans—which made them look more like peasant women than nuns—the Daughters adopted a form of consecrated life that was different from the cloistered model the Council of Trent had insisted upon for women religious several generations earlier. They spent part of their time in prayer and contemplation but also a lot of time roaming about, tending to those in need. This made them resemble tertiaries or members of lay confraternities, so neither Church officials nor French royal officials were prepared to recognize them as a religious order, even though by 1634 they followed a religious rule developed by their foundress.

The Daughters gained official approval slowly and in a piecemeal way. They were approved as a confraternity by the archbishop of Paris in 1646. King Louis XIV then recognized them as a legal entity in 1657. But the pope would not officially recognize them as a secular congregation until 1668—eight years after their foundress' death.

In those days, however, papal approval of new congregations and orders regularly came after, not before, they had a chance to prove their worth to local Catholic lay and clerical authorities. De Marillac thus was able, even without formal approval for many years, to experiment with the Daughters and make of them something not seen before in Catholic consecrated life. The Daughters lived and prayed in community while also going out to serve the poor and the sick in their homes. In time, they served as staff members of hospitals in France, beginning with the Hôtel-Dieu de Paris, the oldest and largest hospital in the French capital. They were invited into different cities and villages around the country to nurture the poor and the sick both bodily and spiritually. They also started orphanages, prison ministries, and schools for girls.

Vincent and Louise encouraged the Daughters to think of themselves as a religious order even though they could not be considered one at the time under the Church's laws. De Paul said of them, "The houses of the sick will be their sole monastery, a rented room their convent cell, the parish church their chapel, the streets their cloister, obedience their enclosure ... the fear of God their convent grille, holy modesty their veil, unceasing confidence in divine providence their vows."[23]

In the decades after Louise's death, the Daughters of Charity became known throughout France. In subsequent centuries, they expanded into mission lands and became one of the most successful congregations in the Church's history. They also served as a model for other women's institutes that were simultaneously contemplative and active. Indeed, despite the early challenges the Daughters faced in gaining official recognition, the form of consecrated life they pioneered in the seventeenth century has become the norm in modern times.

---

23  Joseph Bergin, *Church, Society, and Religious Change in France, 1580–1730* (New Haven, CT: Yale University Press, 2009), 141.

### The devout women of Golden Age France and French North America

The founding of new institutes such as the Daughters of Charity was accompanied by a renewed spirit of piety and charitable activism among French Catholic laywomen in the seventeenth century. Among the figures who stand out in this regard was Antoinette de Pons-Ribérac, the marquess of Guercheville. She was the leading lady-in-waiting to Queen Marie de' Medici, who encouraged other women at the royal court to take a greater interest in charitable service and helped launch the first Jesuit mission to French North America in 1611. Also remarkable was Marie Bonneau de Miramion, a noblewoman who was widowed and left to raise a daughter by herself. She then devoted her life in a radical way—as the foundress of her own congregation—to care for the sick, orphans, and poor girls and young women in need of education and social support.

One of the most impressive Catholic women of the seventeenth century was Marie de Vignerot, the duchess of Aiguillon, who was the fabulously wealthy and politically powerful niece of Cardinal Richelieu, King Louis XIII's prime minister. Vignerot funded and helped organize and develop many of Vincent de Paul's projects within France and abroad in Italy, North Africa, and Madagascar.

A friend also to Louise de Marillac and serving as the president of the Ladies of Charity for two decades, Vignerot helped launch evangelistic missions by French clergy and religious around the world, including in North America and East Asia. She founded, funded, and helped direct numerous new charitable hospitals, religious communities, seminaries and other schools, and ministries for the poor in France and overseas. She also used her wealth and power to encourage good bishops, abbots, and other clergymen in the ongoing

reform and renewal of the Catholic clergy. And she was a tireless patroness of writers and artists who promoted Christian
subjects, including messages about the equal dignity of men
and women in the eyes of God.[24]

Devout Frenchwomen's activities were increasingly global
in scope by the 1630s, thanks in no small part to Vignerot's
labors. Indeed, Vignerot sent across the Atlantic Ocean some
of the first women to serve as Catholic missionaries outside
Europe. These were a group of Canonesses of Saint Augustine
of the Mercy of Jesus, known more commonly as the Hospitalières, whose congregation had been founded in France in
1625. They were devoted in a special way to hospital work.

The Hospitalières were active in French Canada by 1639.
Their task, as stipulated by their lay foundress, was to serve
sick and poor Native Americans at a new charitable hospital
founded just for that purpose. That hospital, the Hôtel-Dieu
du Précieux Sang, was dedicated by Vignerot to "the blood of
the Son of God, shed in order that mercy might be granted
to all men".[25] The Hospitalières were the primary providers
of medical care in the vicinity of Québec in the early colonial period. Given the medical standards of the time, they
were excellent at their work, with exceptionally high cure
rates. They understood their work in spiritual terms too. Each
patient represented God to them, and they also spoke of God
to their patients.

More women came from France to build up charitable
hospital services in colonial North America. One of the first
laywomen to engage in missionary work was Jeanne Mance,
who lived from 1606 to 1673. Becoming skilled in nursing in
France while tending to victims of war and plague during the

24   Bronwen McShea, *La Duchesse: The Life of Marie de Vignerot, Cardinal Richelieu's Forgotten Heiress Who Shaped the Fate of France* (New York: Pegasus Books, 2023).
25   Reuben Gold Thwaites, ed., *The Jesuit Relations and Allied Documents: Travels and Explorations of the Jesuit Missionaries in New France, 1610–1791*, 73 vols. (Cleveland: Burrows Brothers, 1896–1901), 16:25–27.

Thirty Years' War, Mance became involved with a new organization that had formed in Paris, the Société de Notre-Dame de Montréal. The lay and clerical directors of the organization asked Mance to cross the Atlantic to take charge of establishing a new charitable hospital for Native Americans in the vicinity of a new settlement that would grow into the city of Montréal.

Mance devoted the rest of her life to the Hôtel-Dieu de Montréal, which she ran by 1645. Over time, she worked to expand the hospital, traveling back to France to raise money for it and recruiting hospital sisters of a new congregation, the Religious Hospitallers of Saint Joseph, to staff it. The hospital grew considerably over time and long after Mance died in 1673. It was an active hospital until 2017.

In addition to the Frenchwomen who came to colonial Canada to engage in hospital work, other women joined them in the colonial setting as teaching nuns. In 1639, a community of Ursulines arrived on the same ship as the first colonial Hospitalières. They were led by Saint Marie de l'Incarnation, whose name before she entered religious life was Marie Guyart. She was a widow with a young son at the time. The Ursulines of Québec set up a convent and a school, the latter of which was to be focused on the education of Native American girls of Algonquin, Huron, Abenaki, Iroquois, and Montagnais-Naskapi lineage, although students of French ancestry eventually enrolled too.

The Ursulines in Québec taught native and French girls about the Catholic faith, as well as reading, writing, mathematics, and music. They also taught them how to sew and do embroidery, partly so the girls could take such skills into married life, positions in local businesses, or roles as servants in aristocratic homes. Teaching in this vein, the Ursulines of French North America helped maintain a devoutly Catholic as well as urbane tone in a colonial setting that lacked most of the amenities and infrastructure that townspeople in Europe enjoyed at the time.

Over time, the Ursulines and Augustinians in Québec and the Hospitallers of Saint Joseph in Montréal influenced the piety and charitable activities of an array of young Native American women, some of whom wished to take the veil themselves. Unfortunately, indigenous women in the French colonies were prohibited from entering religious life. This was the case for Saint Kateri Tekakwitha, who—along with other contemporary native women who were Catholic—offered her virginity, prayers, and penitential and charitable activities to God while remaining a laywoman.[26]

### Kateri Tekakwitha, Native American virgin-ascetic

Kateri Tekakwitha was born in 1656 in the Iroquois village of Ossernenon—the same village in present-day upstate New York where Saint Isaac Jogues, the Jesuit missionary, had been martyred a decade earlier. She was the daughter of a Mohawk warrior and an Algonquin mother who had been captured by the Mohawks during wartime. Sadly, at the age of four, she was one of only a small number in her village—and the only one in her family—to survive a smallpox epidemic that hit the region. Smallpox left her with vision problems and facial scars that occasioned mistreatment by others as she grew up.

By age ten, Tekakwitha was living with relatives in the village of Caughnawaga, along the Mohawk River, where Jesuit missionaries were active. She received instruction in the Catholic faith and was baptized into the Church on Easter Sunday of 1676 when she was about nineteen.

In the meantime, Tekakwitha was under pressure to get married. But she kept refusing potential husbands as she grew fervent in her faith. This, combined with her vision problems

---

26  Allan Greer, *Mohawk Saint: Catherine Tekakwitha and the Jesuits* (Oxford, UK: Oxford University Press, 2005), 147.

and scars, led to her being socially rejected in Caughnawaga. Realizing she needed more social support to live the life she desired—one of intentional celibacy, prayer, penitence, and charity—she headed north toward Québec, where there was a growing population of Native American Catholics. The largest community of these natives was a fortified mission village called Kahnawaké by the natives and Sault-Saint-Louis by the French. This became her home in the fall of 1677.

At Kahnawaké, Tekakwitha pursued her vocation more fully, in part because there were other native women there who chose not to marry. Among them was Marie-Thérèse Tegaianguenta, who became Tekakwitha's dear friend. The two prayed at times before the large public cross in Kahnawaké and before the Blessed Sacrament in the mission chapel. Tekakwitha joyfully received her first Holy Communion in that chapel at Christmastime in 1677.

Although the Jesuits discouraged Tekakwitha's desire to become a nun, they supported her concern for the sick and the elderly and her decision to make a private promise to God that she would remain a virgin. One of the missionaries, Father Pierre Cholenec, recorded this event in a journal:

> It was the Feast of the Annunciation, March 25, 1679, at eight in the morning, that [Tekakwitha], a moment after Jesus Christ gave Himself in Communion, gave herself totally to Him, and by renouncing marriage forever, she promised perpetual virginity. Then, with a heart all afire with His love, she asked Him to be her only spouse and to take her as His spouse in return. She prayed to Our Lady for whom she had a tender affection [and] consecrated herself to Mary, asking her resolutely to be her mother.[27]

---

27   Pierre Cholenec, S.J., *Catherine Tekakwitha: Her Life,* trans. William Lonc, S.J. (Madison: University of Wisconsin–Madison Press, 2002), 49.

Tekakwitha did not live much longer after this. She had always been frail, and around this time, she contracted a fever and suffered stomach problems. Father Cholenec reported that by Holy Week in 1680 she was approaching death but that her final days seemed to be "days of grace and holiness, because she spent them in living [the] virtues [of] faith ... hope ... charity, humility, gentleness, patience, resignation, and a surprising joyfulness in the midst of her suffering". She died on April 17, 1680, the Wednesday of Holy Week, after speaking the names of Jesus and Mary as her last words.[28]

Cholenec and others reported a miracle shortly after Tekakwitha died: the scars on her face disappeared. The Jesuits and others who knew her were convinced she had gone straight to Heaven, and they encouraged devotion to her as a saint. Various native and French-colonial Catholics thereafter reported miraculous healings and even visions connected to her intercession. In the visions, she always carried a cross and was surrounded by a bright light. Despite this, and despite efforts throughout the Americas to accelerate her cause for sainthood, it was not until World War II that she was declared Venerable in Rome. She was later beatified by Pope John Paul II in 1980 and canonized by Pope Benedict XVI in 2012—making her the first Native American woman to be raised to the honors of the altar.

## Women and the buildup of the Church in the early colonial era

The contributions of Tekakwitha and other Catholic women to the buildup of the Church in French North America are just some of many of the early colonial era. Numerous Catholic

---

28  Ibid., 45–46.

women contributed to the Church's life in colonial Spanish and Portuguese contexts, too, although the circumstances of the Church in such settings differed from those in Canada.

For example, the places into which Spain and Portugal expanded imperially saw far more immigration from Europe. Also, cities such as Mexico City, Lima in Peru, and Manila across the Pacific in the Philippines became metropolises that were, in many ways, reproductions of cities in Spain itself. For this reason, monasteries and convents were established early in the Spanish colonial period. Colonial convents were typically seen, as was the case in Spain, as homes for women from elite families. The nuns in them were expected to live a cloistered life, sometimes to educate Spanish colonial girls, and not to go out into the streets to help the poor or the sick or to evangelize. It was a given, in most cases, that women of any known indigenous or African ancestry would not be permitted entrance except in servile roles. Some of these women who cooked, cleaned, and gardened for the nuns were owned by the communities as slaves.

In view of this, the story of the first Poor Clares community in the Philippines is significant. The foundress was Sister Jerónima de la Asunción. Born in 1555 in Spain, she entered the Poor Clares at age fifteen. Remarkably, almost five decades later, when she was sixty-four and had already dedicated years to reforming her order in Spain, she volunteered to travel halfway across the world to establish a convent in Manila.

Sister Jerónima and six Poor Clares traveled to the Philippines by way of Mexico, arriving in the summer of 1621. Once in Manila, Sister Jerónima labored to build up the Poor Clares in the colonial setting, despite struggling with illness and old age. She died in 1630, three years before a young Filipina whom she had influenced became the first indigenous woman of the Philippines to become a Poor Clare, taking the religious name Marta de San Bernardo.

Colonial authorities in Manila had opposed allowing the Poor Clares to welcome indigenous women such as Marta as professed nuns, but Marta did not take this sitting down. With the support of other Poor Clares, she convinced the minister general of the Franciscans to back her cause. Though she was not allowed to join the order in Manila, where she had hoped to serve as a bridge between her people and the Church in the Philippines, she was able to join in Portuguese Macau in China. She became involved in missionary work near Macau and died around 1650.[29] Furthermore, when some of the prejudice against her people had abated, she inspired other Filipinas in later eras to become nuns and missionaries in their homeland.

### Rose of Lima, first canonized saint from the Americas

The most famous Catholic woman of the Spanish colonial world is Saint Rose of Lima, who lived from 1586 to 1617 and who was canonized in 1671—making her the first canonized saint to have been born in the Americas. Rose was inspired as a child by the example of Saint Catherine of Siena. Raised in a noble family in the city of Lima, which was the capital of the Spanish viceroyalty of Peru, she fasted a lot as a child and, when old enough to receive male attention, cut off her hair and even burned her face to discourage suitors. Resisting her family's efforts to find a husband for her, she spent many hours before the Blessed Sacrament and hoped to consecrate her virginity to Christ as a Dominican nun. When her father refused to let her become a nun, she compromised with him by becoming a lay tertiary when she was twenty.

Rose spent long hours in prayer, sometimes engaging in extreme forms of corporal mortification, such as sleeping on

---

29   D. R. M. Irving, *Colonial Counterpoint: Music in Early Modern Manila* (Oxford, UK: Oxford University Press, 2010), 176–77.

rocks and wearing a spiked silver crown beneath her veil in imitation of Christ's Crown of Thorns. Priests and family members alike tried to curb these behaviors. At the same time, Rose assisted the sick and hungry in her neighborhood. She cared for all kinds of people, including marginalized indigenous and black people. In this, she worked with two male Dominican friends, Saints Juan Macias and Martin de Porres. Miraculous healings were reported in connection with this work.

All this was strange behavior for a young woman in colonial Peru. Many were inspired by Rose's example, however, to the point that after she died at only thirty-one, her funeral was held in Lima's great cathedral and attended by prominent officials. She was canonized about fifty years after her death, partly due to mounting reports of miracles connected to her intercession, including roses falling from the sky and the city of Lima smelling like roses. Rose today is venerated in the Church as the patron saint of the Americas, of Peru and several other countries, and—with Kateri Tekakwitha—of the indigenous peoples of the Americas.

## Chapter 4

# The Enlightenment and Revolutionary Era

The reform, renewal, and expansion of the Church in the early modern era bore fruit in unexpected ways. By 1665, for example, a seminary training indigenous men for the priesthood had been established in the kingdom of Ayutthaya in what is present-day Thailand, thanks partly to the enterprising labors of the duchess of Aiguillon and her friends in Paris. Additionally, a woman well known to that circle, Louise de La Vallière, was moved to change her life and become a Discalced Carmelite in the early 1670s after leading a sinful life as King Louis XIV's mistress. Mother to four of the king's children, she had to fight Louis' desire to keep her at court but eventually spent thirty-five years in a convent and produced a beautiful memoir about her journey out of sin.

In the seventeenth and eighteenth centuries, numerous seminaries were founded to train the clergy, and Catholic schools multiplied for younger students too, including, increasingly, for girls and young women. Catholic hospitals, orphanages, and other charitable institutions were founded, and those who staffed them—often consecrated women—sometimes demonstrated the most advanced nursing, pharmaceutical, and administrative skills seen in the era.

At the same time, the Church faced unprecedented challenges. In European cities such as Paris, London, and Vienna, new modes of thinking and writing about philosophy, the sciences, and social life emerged, encouraging people to question all manner of traditional ways of understanding and engaging with the world. Influential voices in this period, called the Enlightenment era, urged people to disregard Christian claims about miracles and the supernatural. In France, especially, writers targeted the Church and especially her clergy and monastics. Additionally, prominent leaders within the Church, such as Holy Roman Emperor Joseph II—who co-ruled for a time with one of the most powerful Catholic women in history, his mother, Empress Maria Theresa—caused new rifts among Catholics with efforts to subordinate the clergy, schools, and charitable institutions to monarchical states.

By the late eighteenth century, revolutions favoring liberal and democratic principles unfolded in what became the young United States of America, in France, and in other countries. In France, the violence moved in shocking directions, not only toppling a monarchy that had been in place for thirteen centuries but also resulting in the slaughter of Catholic clergymen, religious, and laypeople who favored the traditional order. Religious orders were suppressed not only in revolutionary France but also in the Holy Roman Empire and other parts of Europe influenced by the policies of Joseph II, and there was a massive transfer of ecclesiastical properties to secular states.

Catholic leaders, in short, were suddenly at a crossroads, debating how best to protect the Church and to restore her unity, institutions, and public authority amid the tumult. Unexpectedly, some answers for how to proceed would emerge in unlikely places, such as the United States of America and revolutionary France, where women played as vital a role in preserving and advancing Catholic worship, faith, and social witness as they had in past times of crisis.

### Religious pioneers of formal education for girls

One of the most important developments in early modern Europe was the buildup of formal educational institutions for girls as well as boys, much of it pioneered by consecrated women. Religious women had earlier been some of the first providers of formal schooling for girls, as we saw in the cases of Saint Angela Merici and the Ursulines, as well as Mary Ward and the Sisters of Loreto.

Convent-based schools for girls run by the Ursulines and other new congregations began to proliferate in Europe in the seventeenth century and began to appear overseas in French, Spanish, and Portuguese colonies. Additionally, Catholic schools were permitted to operate in Protestant England and included several schools for girls established by the Sisters of Loreto—institutions that frequently faced harassment by government officials. By the end of the eighteenth century, the still-prestigious New Hall School in Essex, which today is coeducational, was run by the Canonesses Regular of the Holy Sepulchre, an order first active in what is today Belgium.

Nearby in Ireland, which English and Scottish Protestants had colonized, marginalizing the Catholic majority, consecrated women devoted their lives to educating poor girls and boys alike. Among them were Nano Nagle in Cork, the foundress of the Sisters of the Presentation of the Blessed Virgin Mary, who ran five schools for girls by 1769. In time, Nagle worked with Teresa Mulally, a laywoman and philanthropist who had started a small school and then boardinghouse for poor Catholic girls in Dublin. Nagle's congregation eventually took over these institutions.[1]

By the turn of the nineteenth century, schools for girls run by consecrated women were enough of a norm that new institutes began to be established specifically to advance girls' education. This was true of the Religious of the Sacred Heart of Jesus established in France in 1800 by Saint Madeleine Sophie Barat. The Sacred Heart sisters first opened a free school for

---

1    Rosemary Raughter, "A Discreet Benevolence: Female Philanthropy and the Catholic Resurgence in Eighteenth-Century Ireland", *Women's History Review* 6, no. 4 (1997): 468.

poor girls in the French city of Amiens and eventually opened similar schools elsewhere in France. Soon after, Saint Rose Philippine Duchesne and other Sacred Heart sisters started free schools across the Atlantic in the young United States. Sacred Heart schools also opened in other countries, providing an education that was both intellectually and spiritually nourishing, as well as useful to girls of little economic means because it taught them skills that employers valued.

### The first Catholic women in higher education

Although attention increasingly was paid to educating girls in the seventeenth and eighteenth centuries, women remained generally forbidden from enrolling in institutions of higher learning or training in professions such as law and medicine. It was virtually unthinkable that they could become university-based scholars and professors in any field. This makes the few early exceptions all the more remarkable.

Seven of the nine women known to have earned advanced degrees in the early modern era were Catholics in Italy and Spain. The first was Elena Lucrezia Cornaro Piscopia, who earned a doctorate in philosophy at the University of Padua in 1678, several years after becoming a Benedictine oblate privately vowed to chastity. Piscopia, who was thirty-two at the time of this unprecedented achievement, was a prodigy. In the preceding years, after demonstrating exceptional intellectual acuity as a girl, she had mastered Spanish, French, Latin, Greek, Hebrew, and Aramaic, and she had studied mathematics, music, philosophy, and theology at advanced levels.

While her musical abilities were much admired, Piscopia was drawn to theology under the influence of her tutor, Carlo Rinaldini, who taught philosophy at Padua and encouraged her to translate into Italian a Spanish treatise on Christ by a monk named Lanspergius. Rinaldi then tried to welcome Piscopia into the theology department at Padua, but the local cardinal-archbishop, Gregorio Barbarigo, objected to granting a theology degree to a woman. This is why she received a doctorate in philosophy instead.

More than half a century passed before another woman, Laura Maria Caterina Bassi, received a doctoral degree. With the support of the future Pope Benedict XIV, Bassi went on to teach physics at the University of Bologna after earning a PhD in the field in 1732. She was also elected to the Academy of Sciences of the Institute of Bologna. In her lectures, she encouraged other scientists to take Newtonian physics more seriously, as they were still focused on some of the teachings of Galen and Descartes.[2] Bassi married a professor of medicine named Giuseppe Veratti, and the two supported each other's intellectual work and raised at least eight children.

Bassi paved the way at Bologna for another Italian woman, Cristina Roccati, to receive her PhD in physics in 1751. Roccati was tutored by a seminary rector who recognized her intellectual gifts. By age fifteen, she was encouraged by him to enroll at the University of Bologna, where Bassi was lecturing. Roccati became as celebrated for writing poetry as for her abilities in physics and other sciences. She was elected to several academic societies and went on to study at an advanced level at the University of Padua. She also taught Newtonian physics for many years at the Academy of Concordia in Rovigo.

Other Catholic women who were pioneers for women in higher education include Maria Pellegrina Amoretti, a northern Italian who was the first woman to receive a doctor of laws degree, which she did at the University of Pavia in 1777 when she was twenty, and Maria Dalle Donne, who received

---

2   Monique Frize, *Laura Bassi and Science in 18th Century Europe: The Extraordinary Life and Role of Italy's Pioneering Female Professor* (Heidelberg, DE: Springer, 2013).

a doctorate in medicine at the University of Bologna in 1799. Dalle Donne defended several theses publicly, with great acclaim, inside the Church of San Domenico. She also worked as a physician and university director in Bologna.

In Spain, María Pascuala Caro Sureda, who studied at the University of Valencia, received a PhD in 1779. Two years later she published a work in physics and mathematics entitled *Ensayo de Historía, Física y Matemáticas*, and in 1789, she became a Dominican nun in Mallorca, where she eventually served as her convent's prioress. Another Spanish woman, María Isidra de Guzmán y de la Cerda, received a PhD at the University of Alcalà and was made an honorary member of the university's faculty. Elected to several academic and royal societies, including Spain's Royal Academy of History, she was respected for her philosophical work and her translations from Latin into Spanish.

### Other learned Catholic women of the Enlightenment era

Other early modern Catholic women pursued higher learning and contributed to intellectual debates of the period, including Juana Inés de la Cruz, a remarkable woman who lived in colonial Mexico from 1648 to 1695. Although she was the illegitimate daughter of a Spanish colonial nobleman, she received an excellent education by spending time in her grandfather's library. Fluent at a young age in Latin, the indigenous language Nahuatl, and her Spanish mother tongue, she composed a poem on the Eucharist by the age of eight, studied Greek logic at home, and began teaching Latin to others when she was a teenager.

De la Cruz loved learning so much that she disguised herself as a boy when she was sixteen so that she could attempt to study at the university in Mexico City. This did not work out, but she became known for her learning all the same at the court of the colonial viceroy and was able to pursue high-level scholarship and writing as a nun of the Hieronymite order. Her cell inside the convent of Santa Paula in Mexico City became a salon, a place where well-educated women visited to learn from her and discuss ideas. However, when she was forty-two, controversy swirled around her after the bishop of Puebla published a critique she had written of a particular sermon by a Portuguese Jesuit named António Vieira. The bishop did this without asking her and attached the pen name Sor Filotea to it. The bishop then published his own criticism of her work and Vieira's.

After the bishop suggested that, as a woman in a convent, the learned nun should remain silent and devoted to prayer, Juana penned a defense of a woman's right to receive an education, to write, and to publish. She argued, furthermore, that women should be put in positions of authority to teach other women so that no scandalous business between male teachers and female students would transpire. The archbishop of Mexico condemned her for this. She stopped writing in 1693, two years before dying of the plague, which she caught while tending to others who had contracted it. By then, she had written many poems, dramas, comedies, and works of philosophy, and she had also composed music. One of her poems was written in Nahuatl and concerned the Our Lady of Guadalupe, who had appeared to Saint Juan Diego two centuries earlier.

Another learned woman of the era was María de Guadalupe de Lencastre, the duchess of Aveiro, to whom we were introduced in the previous chapter. This Portuguese noblewoman lived from 1630 to 1715 and, sadly, had an unhappy marriage. Her husband, a Spanish duke, divorced her over a dispute regarding land she had inherited from her parents. Amid such difficulties, the duchess became famous for her erudition and ability to converse with leading thinkers about scientific developments and intellectual debates of the time. She also became known as a patroness of the arts and a skilled painter herself. But she is best remembered for her support of the Jesuits' overseas missions—something she pursued when other European elites were flagging in their commitment to such causes.[3]

Learned women were increasingly celebrated in eighteenth-century Spain. For example, Josefa Amar y Borbón, the highly educated daughter of a prominent physician, was the first woman to be elected to the Aragonese Economic Society and was then welcomed into the prestigious Madrid Economic Society. Amar lived from 1749 to 1833 and produced a controversial work titled *Discourse on the Talent of Women*, in which she argued—several years before the famous English feminist Mary Wollstonecraft made a similar argument— "that if women received the same education as men, they would achieve as much or more than they do". Unlike Wollstonecraft, Amar grounded her view of men and women's "intellectual equality" in Christianity, especially her reading of Genesis.[4]

## Maria Theresa of Austria, ruler of the Habsburg domains and Church reformer

One of the most powerful figures in the Enlightenment era was a pious Catholic mother of sixteen children, Empress Maria Theresa of Austria, the only woman ever to rule over the Holy Roman Empire and the other domains controlled by the Habsburg dynasty. She fulfilled this unprecedented role

---

3    Jeanne Gillespie, "Casting New Molds: The Duchess of Aveiro's Global Colonial Enterprise (1669–1715)", *Early Modern Women* 8 (2013): 301–15.

4    Ulrich L. Lehner and Shaun Blanchard, eds., *The Catholic Enlightenment: A Global Anthology* (Washington, DC: The Catholic University of America Press, 2021), 103, 98.

for a woman between 1740 and 1780. Her reign was consequential for the Church and for European politics and culture.

Through intermarriages with Europe's royal families over the centuries, the Habsburg imperial family had by the eighteenth century come to dominate the kingdoms of Bohemia (today part of the Czech Republic), Hungary, Croatia, Galicia, Portugal, and Spain. It also controlled principalities in the Netherlands and for a time ruled Mexico, Brazil, Austria, the rest of the Holy Roman Empire, and other lands overseas. Thus, to be born into the imperial family in Vienna came with tremendous responsibilities, especially if one happened to be the likely successor of the reigning emperor, who also was the sovereign of Austria and of other kingdoms and principalities.

This was the destiny of Maria Theresa Walburga Amalia Christina von Habsburg, born on May 13, 1717, to Emperor Charles VI and Empress Elisabeth of Brunswick-Wolfenbüttel. Charles had sadly lost a son and heir, Leopold, a year before, and although he hoped for another son, he faced the prospect of one day passing on his vast domains, in an unprecedented way for the Habsburgs, to an heiress instead of an heir. Indeed, the emperor and his wife went on to have two more daughters but no more sons. So, from a young age, Maria Theresa was the heir apparent.

Charles resented this, however. He did not provide Maria Theresa the full education that befitted her future position of public responsibility. She was forbidden from learning horsemanship, for example—a skill she would need when reviewing troops as the commander of the imperial armies. Also, though she was tutored in Latin and other subjects by Jesuits, she was not taught at an advanced level. She was, instead, urged to focus on drawing, painting, music, dancing, and etiquette. Eventually, however, Charles let Maria Theresa attend meetings with his royal council, which enabled her to absorb some political knowledge and to observe her father's style as a ruler.

As Maria Theresa grew up, she proved to be pretty, healthy, and intelligent. She had large blue eyes, light hair with a reddish tint, and a strong body in an age when it was fashionable for aristocratic girls to appear frail. She absorbed knowledge quickly and was simultaneously reserved and amiable. She loved archery and singing and even performed in operas at court.

The question of Maria Theresa's marriage was of primary importance to her family and the empire. She was relieved when, at age eighteen, a marriage was arranged between her and Francis Stephen, a young man for whom she already had fond feelings. Francis Stephen was the heir to the sovereign duke of Lorraine and grand duke of Tuscany and was in his midtwenties.

Unfortunately, Francis Stephen proved to be an unfaithful spouse. At the same time, he became an effective political partner to his wife, who inherited her father's domains unexpectedly when she was still quite young. Charles died at only fifty-eight, and Maria Theresa came to power at twenty-three.

Although imperial law technically forbade any woman from wearing the crown of the Holy Roman Empire—the crown was instead placed on Francis Stephen's head—Maria Theresa was the de facto ruler of the empire, and Francis Stephen served her loyally in the role of a consort. He handled the empire's financial affairs but did not try to assert himself as the sovereign. His wife fulfilled the responsibilities of her position, even during many periods of pregnancy and mourning the death of her children. Between 1737 and 1756, Maria Theresa gave birth to eleven daughters and five sons, six of whom died very young.

Despite her youth, Maria Theresa impressed seasoned statesmen and proved to be an effective, reform-minded ruler. She became famous for reforming governmental and financial institutions, the military, medicine, education, commerce, and agriculture. Enlightenment-era ideas about bureaucratic centralization, rationalized organization, and efficiency were often applied in these efforts.

At the same time, Maria Theresa opposed some new ideas being advanced by liberal thinkers. Most notably, she did not believe that religious diversity was good for her empire. She thus encouraged efforts to convert Protestants to Catholicism within her domains. Furthermore, she believed that Church and state should be firmly united. However, this did not mean that Church officials were to control political affairs. Rather, in a state that was becoming more bureaucratized, stronger, and more centralized, Maria Theresa and other royal officials increasingly controlled ecclesiastical institutions and properties within the Habsburg domains. The imperial state selected and oversaw many of the men who became bishops and supervised Catholic hospitals, orphanages, and schools, including seminaries.

In contrast, monasteries and estates owned by religious orders remained relatively independent of state control under this system—something that frustrated Maria Theresa and many bishops in her service. Indeed, religious orders traditionally enjoyed exemptions from episcopal control due to both historic and current arrangements with the papacy. Maria Theresa thus sympathized with reform-minded Catholics who were aligned with a movement known as Jansenism, which favored nationalizing the Church and sought to empower state-employed bishops in new ways in relation to both the papacy and the larger body of the faithful.

Related to this, Maria Theresa had a complicated relationship with the Jesuits. She had been educated by Jesuits, had Jesuit confessors, and preferred Jesuits as educators for her son, the future Emperor Joseph II. However, as her reign went on, the Jesuits were increasingly seen as too favorable to the papacy and resistant to her reforms. Various powerful people in her government—some of them bishops—convinced her that the Jesuits threatened the state. So, by the 1760s, she began removing Jesuits from positions of influence in her empire.[5]

Maria Theresa furthermore favored reforms of the Church's public culture that were seen by some of her fellow Catholics as modern and problematic. For example, she reduced the number of public religious holidays, partly for the sake of bringing economic relief to the poor. And, late in her reign, she and her son Joseph, who co-ruled with her from 1765 to 1780, subordinated monasteries and convents to bishops to an unprecedented degree in parts of her empire.[6]

One of the darker aspects of Maria Theresa's reign is the anti-Semitism her government promoted. Early in her reign, the empress promoted the expulsion of Jews from different parts of her empire. Later, however, she softened her position due to the influence of Abraham Mendel Theben, a Hungarian Jewish leader who convinced her to change some of her policies.

Maria Theresa's record with respect to Eastern Rite Catholics and Eastern Orthodox Christians merits mention. With respect to Eastern Rite Catholics, the empress ensured that they were not treated as second-class citizens alongside the majority of Latin Rite Catholics. With respect to Serbians, Romanians, and other Eastern Orthodox Christians who were not in communion with the pope, Maria Theresa extended a friendly hand. Eastern Orthodox communities living just beyond the borders of her empire in the east and southeast were guaranteed protection. There was a strategic purpose to this: Maria Theresa wanted to win over Orthodox populations living beyond her empire's border in lands controlled by the declining Ottoman Empire so she could grow her empire

---

5    Barbara Stollberg-Rilinger, *Maria Theresa: The Habsburg Empress in Her Time*, trans. Robert Savage (Princeton, NJ: Princeton University Press, 2022), 591–92.
6    Ibid.

there. Indeed, her Kingdom of Hungary eventually absorbed Serbian lands previously claimed by the Ottomans.

### Marie Antoinette, victim of the French Revolution

Empress Maria Theresa is as famous because of who her children were as because of her own career. Her heir, Emperor Joseph II, was one of the most controversial rulers of the late eighteenth century, in part because of his aggressive efforts to subordinate Catholic institutions to the imperial state, even more fully than his mother had done. He was especially opposed to contemplative religious orders that were not engaged in "useful" educational and social-charitable work, and he dissolved at least six hundred monasteries and convents throughout his domains. He did this with the support of Catholic bishops several years before revolutionaries would follow suit in France.

Even more famous among Maria Theresa's children was Marie Antoinette, who was the queen of France when the French Revolution broke out in 1789. On October 16, 1793, she was publicly guillotined in Paris, just months after her husband, King Louis XVI, was toppled from power and executed in the same way.

The executions of the Catholic monarch of France and his Austrian-born queen constituted one of the most important turning points in the history of the Church since the Reformation. Considering what led to this event from Marie Antoinette's vantage point helps us understand why.

Growing up at her mother's court in Vienna, the young princess was steeped in Catholic piety, as well as the magnificent sacred art and music of the era that her parents and other elites in the Habsburg domains patronized. She was also taught by her mother and other ladies at court to prepare for a life as a dutiful consort to whichever prince she would marry—the identity of whom was clear by 1770, when Marie Antoinette was fourteen. That year, she was sent from her homeland to marry the sixteen-year-old grandson and heir of King Louis XV of France. The two young people had an awkward time with married life at first because they had been introduced to each other only two days before their wedding. Additionally, the future Louis XVI was shy and interested more in scientific experiments than in his bride. Louis also had legitimate concerns that if he were to grow close to her, the Habsburg family would dominate him once he was king.

It took eight years for Marie Antoinette to become a mother; a healthy daughter, Marie-Thérèse, was born in 1778. By then, Louis and Marie Antoinette had been the king and queen of France for four years. Three other children followed: Louis-Joseph, who should have been his father's heir but who suffered from tuberculosis and died in childhood; Louis-Charles, a healthier boy; and Sophie, who sadly died less than a year after her birth, also of tuberculosis.

Marie Antoinette was a devoted mother, and over time she and King Louis grew very fond of each other. But early in their marriage, the queen fell in love with a Swedish count, Axel von Fersen, who fought in the American Revolution, which the French were supporting against Britain. This caused suffering for all involved. It is unclear how far the queen and the count acted upon their romantic feelings for each other. Louis XVI, for his part, was faithful to his wife.

Residing at the magnificent Palace of Versailles twenty miles outside Paris, Marie Antoinette enjoyed continual rounds of parties and other diversions alongside most of the upper nobility of France. In that period, most higher-level nobles, including many cardinals and bishops, resided at court. Their domains, meanwhile, were often mismanaged by deputies, as France generally was supported by the labor of peasants, artisans, and shopkeepers, as well as by merchants, lawyers, and other professionals who shouldered most of the tax burden.

Partly because of long-standing problems in the French tax system and partly because of the debt the kingdom incurred assisting the Americans against Britain, some officials in Louis XVI's government favored reforms, including the elimination of tax exemptions enjoyed by many nobles and by the Church, which possessed about 6 percent of the kingdom's land. The king was sympathetic with some reform ideas and in 1789 called together an unusual meeting called the Estates General. This was a gathering of representatives of the common people, the clergy, and the nobility of a kind that had not occurred since 1614.

Some of the representatives who came to the Estates General in Paris in the spring of 1789 supported the liberalization of French political institutions. They wanted a permanent representative body similar to the English Parliament that would be able to make laws with the Crown, and they wanted freedom of the press and the elimination of most privileges for nobles, such as being the only people permitted to serve as military officers or high-level Church officials. They also wanted the Church in France to become fully joined to the state, with priests serving dually as civil servants and pastors, and with monks and nuns engaged only in "useful" work such as school teaching and tending to the sick.

While nobles and royal officials supported some of these ideas, events in 1789 led to a revolutionary act: the representatives of the common people who had been called to participate in the Estates General declared themselves, illegally, to be the new National Assembly of France and began issuing laws, such as the abolition of all noble privileges and the confiscation of monastic lands, in the name of the French people. Violence then broke out in Paris when the king tried to stop them.

Events spiraled out of control. Liberals and radicals favored the National Assembly, while more traditional-minded elites—including Marie Antoinette and her circle—pressed the king to call in military assistance from France's allies to reverse the revolutionary actions. Although the king and queen were still in power, they could not stop the revolutionary decisions being made in their name and that of the French people. So, in June 1791, they attempted to flee the country with their children to secure assistance from Emperor Leopold II, the second of the queen's brothers to rule the Holy Roman Empire.

The royal family members, however, were discovered before they reached the eastern border and were put under surveillance while the National Assembly crafted a constitution for France. The king accepted the constitution, but the revolutionary government failed to maintain order and the country descended into violence between radicals and traditionalists. The latter entirely opposed the revolution, and the former were increasingly anti-monarchical and anti-Catholic, favoring the complete elimination of the kingdom's ancient institutions.

The radicals succeeded in taking over the revolution. They worked to overthrow the monarchy and banish from France all clergymen, including bishops, who did not accept an unprecedented program that forced the Church to submit to the arbitrary decisions of the revolutionary legislature. While that legislature claimed to represent the French people, most peasants and other commoners throughout the country were piously Catholic and conservative. France thus descended into civil war as the king and queen continued secretly to stir up opposition to the revolution through contacts abroad. An international war against the revolutionaries broke out by the spring of 1792.

By August 13, 1792, the king and queen and their two surviving children were being held as prisoners in Paris. A few weeks later, killings known as the September Massacres resulted in the deaths of more than two hundred priests, many nuns and brothers, and innumerable laypeople—possibly as many as 1,600 people altogether—throughout the French capital. Some of these killings occurred inside a Carmelite monastery. Louis XVI was eventually tried and convicted by the new National Convention for alleged crimes against his own people. He was executed with a guillotine late in the morning on January 21, 1793.

The devastated queen remained under house arrest with her daughter and son. In July, however, Louis-Charles, who was only eight and who was the rightful king of France, was taken from her and locked in a different cell, fed very little, and abused by the prison guards. He was coerced into accusing his own mother and an aunt of having sexually molested him—something that broke Marie Antoinette's heart. This boy died several years later from a combination of tuberculosis and the cruelties to which he had been subjected.

On August 3, 1793, the queen was taken from her daughter, Marie-Thérèse, and was thrown into the Conciergerie prison in Paris. There she was visited in her small, dark cell by a priest, and she prayed often before a crucifix, sometimes with the aid of *The Imitation of Christ*, one of two books she was permitted to have. She, too, was then condemned as an enemy of the French people and beheaded on October 19. She was thirty-seven. Marie-Thérèse, who cried often for her mother, was not told about any of this for almost two years.

Marie Antoinette's execution had been ordered by the most radical revolutionaries who had taken control of the government in the spring of 1793. These Jacobins, as they were called, inaugurated a period in French history remembered as the Reign of Terror. Thousands of people—including clergymen, monks, and nuns—were killed. Anyone who demonstrated sympathy for the royal family or the traditional Church was suspected of treason. The Jacobins took over churches, including Notre Dame Cathedral, and forced a state-approved, paganistic, and Enlightenment-friendly religion on the people, who largely wished to maintain the Catholic faith of their ancestors. They also desecrated the graves of past monarchs of France.

This phase of the revolution—including the murder of the queen—caused such horror among so many people that a successful counterrevolution took place in the summer of 1794. Retaliatory violence from all sides continued to unfold, however, and a young, ambitious general who favored the revolution, Napoleon Bonaparte, proved to be the only person capable of returning order to the country. Bonaparte declared himself to be the emperor of the French, and his policies and military conquests across Europe caused many new problems, including for the Church.

After Napoleon, too, was eventually deposed, the traditional monarchy of France was temporarily restored and Catholicism was once again made the state religion. During that period, Marie Antoinette's cell at the Conciergerie was turned into a chapel. And by that point, Catholics across Europe were deeply divided over whether to accept the new liberal tendencies that had taken root in various countries or to restore the traditional order that had existed in the days when Marie Antoinette was a young princess.

### Women who resisted French revolutionary radicalism

The best-known women who resisted the French Revolution are, unsurprisingly, the most high-profile women, such as Marie Antoinette and a high-ranking courtier named Béatrix de Choiseul-Stainville, the duchess of Gramont, who ran a literary salon before the revolution. Although such women often went to Mass and were leading members of the Church in France, they are not remembered for their sterling morality. Choiseul-Stainville was proud and ambitious and even attempted to become Louis XV's official mistress at one point. As an older woman, however, she refused to tell an untruth to save her life. Put on trial during the Reign of Terror, she answered boldly when asked if she risked her life to help other people targeted by the new regime to escape from France, admitting to the "crime" of which she was accused. She was guillotined soon after in July 1794.

Some brave Frenchwomen who fought back against the revolutionaries included those who joined counterrevolutionary organizations. Many of these organizations formed in response to the new regime's efforts to force Catholic clergymen and religious to swear oaths of loyalty to the revolutionaries. One such organization was the Association Bretonne, which kindled an uprising in Brittany. An interesting member of this organization was Thérèse de Moëlien, a secret agent connected to other counterrevolutionaries and Catholic resistance leaders. She helped recruit others to her cause but was eventually guillotined at age thirty-four.

A historian named Olwen Hufton has detailed the remarkable efforts of otherwise ordinary Catholic peasant women to protect priests and nuns during the most destructive phases of the revolution. These women were committed to ensuring that the Catholic Mass was properly offered—covertly in their homes if necessary—while regime-approved clergymen performed counterfeit services in churches that had been co-opted by the radicals. Sometimes these women met with arrest and worse. Sometimes enough banded together—even while many of their husbands, sons, and brothers complied with the state—and authorities were forced to back down. Indeed, it was in large part due to the steadfastness of ordinary French Catholic women that the most radical revolutionary measures against the Church were revoked later in the 1790s.

Occasionally such women defended the Church and the Mass in ways that were not terribly saintly but that demonstrated great fidelity. Noteworthy was what happened in the parish of Saint-Vincent in the diocese of Le Puy-en-Velay. Even three hundred miles south of Paris, the radical new regime's functionaries had overthrown the people's beloved Mass. In its place was a regime-approved counterfeit that invoked liberty, reason, and an impersonal deity. In addition, Saint-Vincent had been stripped of its sacred images and objects—many of them lovingly gifted to the parish in years past by laypeople.

The lower-status women of this parish did not take the assault on their sacred space and ancient liturgy sitting down. Instead, they organized. One day, when the whole community was gathered to hear a state-appointed clergyman preach messages of the new regime, he and the compliant, elite members of the community were in for a surprise. As Hufton narrates, "The unlucky celebrant began his patriotic oration when, at a sign from an old woman, the entire female audience rose, turned their backs on the altar of liberty, and raised their skirts to expose their bare buttocks and to express their feelings to the new deity." The clergyman was "reduced to gibberish". He and the local officials sitting toward the front rushed out of the building as the women cast aspersions on their manhood. Hufton further reported that news of this incident led to its replication in other parishes nearby.[7]

## The Carmelite martyrs of Compiègne

Some Catholic women responded to the new regime's attacks on religion in truly saintly ways. Chief among them were nuns and sisters who refused to renounce the vows they had made

---

7    Olwen H. Hufton, *Women and the Limits of Citizenship in the French Revolution* (Toronto: University of Toronto Press, 1992), 118.

to God, even at the price of death. For example, Blessed Marguerite Rutan, a Daughter of Charity who ran a hospital for the poor and engaged in pioneering educational and social work for young girls in southwestern France, was guillotined at age fifty-seven in the town of Dax on April 9, 1794, after refusing to swear an oath of loyalty to the state.

Likewise, a group of Daughters of Charity in Arras in northern France, who remained together to serve the poor after the local bishop and other clergymen in the vicinity had fled the country, also refused to take an oath of loyalty to the new regime when an ex-priest attempted to make them do so. They were arrested, tried, and guillotined on June 26, 1794. Their elderly superior, Blessed Marie-Madeleine Fontaine, declared from the platform before she was killed that Christ's altars would soon rise gloriously again in France.

Additionally, a Poor Clare named Joséphine Leroux, Joséphine's biological sister, two Ursuline mothers, and two Bridgettine nuns were executed in Valenciennes, France, later in 1794.

All these women have been beatified by the Church but await canonization. The same is true of the most famous group of Catholic women who resisted the revolutionary regime in France. This was a community of eleven nuns, three lay sisters, and two tertiaries who are remembered as the Carmelite martyrs of Compiègne. These sixteen Carmelites of all ages refused to disband or renounce the commitments they had made to God, despite tremendous pressure from the revolutionary regime.

Based in the town of Compiègne, northeast of Paris, these women, led by Thérèse de Saint-Augustin, refused to swear an oath of loyalty to the new regime. This led to their arrest in June 1794. Initially, they were imprisoned in a repurposed Visitation convent. They prayed together and encouraged one another to remain steadfast by not submitting to the new regime and to regard their likely executions as a chance to suffer with Christ Crucified, their divine spouse.

Their trial took place in Paris on July 17. They wore their habits, which had been outlawed, to the courtroom. They were quickly condemned as enemies of the French people. Later that same day, they were carted through the streets of Paris to a square (what is today the Place de la Nation) where the dreaded guillotine awaited them. Along the way, the nuns sang the *Salve Regina* ("Hail Holy Queen") and the prayers for Vespers and Compline. A mob that had grown used to cheering on bloody sacrifices to the new gods of Liberty, Equality, and Fraternity was gathered there. Before this crowd, the women renewed their religious vows at the foot of the platform. They then sang the *Te Deum* ("God, We Praise You") and the *Veni Creator Spiritus* ("Come, Holy Spirit").

The first nun to approach the guillotine, young Sister Constance, actually made her first religious profession at this place, as she had been a novice until then. She then knelt and kissed a statue of the Blessed Virgin held by the mother superior, asked permission to die, and chanted the hymn *Laudate Dominum Omnes Gentes* ("O praise the Lord, all you nations") on the platform. Then she calmly placed her neck on the guillotine. All the other Carmelites had joined in the hymn and kept singing as each woman kissed the cross, asked permission to die, and approached death willingly.

The crowd, which usually jeered during executions, went silent as the women sang, their voices slowly reduced to just that of Mother Thérèse, who was the last to embrace death this way.

Ten days later, the Reign of Terror ended with a counter-revolutionary takeover of the government. There is a tradition among French Catholics which maintains that the martyrs of Compiègne, once in Heaven, helped end the worst of the revolution's violence with their intercessions.

## Elizabeth Ann Seton and the Church
## in the young revolutionary United States

On the other side of the Atlantic Ocean, while the French Revolution was raging, a young Episcopalian woman from an Anglo-American family in New York City got married at age nineteen to a wealthy merchant of Scottish ancestry. Her maiden name was Elizabeth Ann Bayley, and her husband's name was William Seton.

Mr. and Mrs. Seton started a family amid the peace and prosperity they enjoyed as elite Protestants in the new United States of America, the revolutionary nation that inspired democratic revolutions across Europe and the Americas but that, for a variety of reasons, suffered less instability than other revolutionary nations. In time, the Setons had five children—three girls and two boys. Their mother took their formation as Episcopalians very seriously and took the time to serve poor families in Manhattan while raising her own.

Sadly, William died of tuberculosis early in the marriage. This proved to be a major turning point in his wife's life, not only because she became a young widow but also because his death unexpectedly led her to discover Catholicism. Seton had brought her husband to Italy shortly before he died in 1803, hoping the climate would help him recover, and she stayed in Italy for several months while in mourning. Though she had been raised with strong anti-Catholic prejudices in New York, she began to encounter Catholicism on its own terms in Italy. And she found herself drawn—in a way that startled her because she did not believe what Catholics do about the Eucharist—to the Blessed Sacrament reserved in tabernacles in beautiful old churches she visited.

Once she was home in Manhattan, Seton experienced turmoil over her interest in Catholicism. Most of her loved ones, who had respectable positions in New York society, regarded it as the superstitious faith of socioeconomic and ethnic groups that were beneath them. However, long conversations with her Episcopalian bishop led Seton to conclude that the Catholic Church was the true Church. In the spring of 1805, when she was thirty years old, she courageously converted.

Seton's conversion earned rebukes from relatives and friends. The next several years in New York proved difficult for the young widow and single mother. She tried to start a boardinghouse to earn income for her family, but parents who contemplated sending their children there reconsidered when they realized Seton was Catholic.

In 1809, she took another great step when she moved her family to Emmitsburg, Maryland, far from everything she knew. Maryland had long been a haven for Catholics. There, she started a free school for girls—Saint Joseph's Academy and Free School—with the assistance of Sulpician priests from France. Seton was now a pioneer of Catholic education in the young and largely Protestant United States.

At this point, Seton felt a tug toward a more radical way of life. She was inspired by her newfound devotion to the Blessed Mother. So she founded a new religious congregation for women, the Sisters of Charity of Saint Joseph's, who by 1811 followed the rule of the Daughters of Charity who had been founded by Saints Louise de Marillac and Vincent de Paul. Seton became the congregation's first mother superior.

Based in Emmitsburg, Seton's Sisters of Charity became the first women's congregation formed in the United States. There were nineteen professed members by mid-1813. They initially focused on teaching at the free school but soon opened an orphanage in Philadelphia and became active in Seton's hometown of New York as well.

As she was developing these ministries, Seton suffered the loss of two of her daughters to tuberculosis—the same disease that had killed their father. Tragically, Seton herself contracted tuberculosis and died on January 4, 1821, when she was only forty-six.

Regarded as saintly by many who knew her, Seton was beatified less than forty years after she died and was canonized in Rome in 1975. This was a festive occasion for American Catholics, as Seton was the first US citizen to be declared a saint of the Church.[8]

Daughters of Charity who traced their lineage to Seton's first community, as well as numerous other consecrated women, were critical to the emergence of Catholic schools all over the young United States. A need for such schools grew as it became clear that America's taxpayer-funded schools would generally promote Protestant views, even after Catholic laypeople and clergy asked for a more Catholic-inclusive approach.

Among the congregations devoted to teaching were Ursulines, who had been active in Louisiana since the era of French colonialism and who ran Catholic schools for girls across the country by the early twentieth century. Also active were sisters of Madeleine Sophie Barat's Religious of the Sacred Heart of Jesus. In 1818, eight years before this French congregation was approved in Rome, Saint Rose Philippine Duchesne from Grenoble led a group of Sacred Heart sisters across the Atlantic and started a school in Saint Charles, Missouri, deep in the American Midwest. This was before Missouri was a state. Sacred Heart sisters would go on to open schools for girls in many states, including Ohio, Nebraska, Pennsylvania, and Connecticut.

Religious women proved to be essential to the moral, social, and intellectual formation of a significant Catholic population across the ever-expanding American republic.

---

8    Catherine O'Donnell, *Elizabeth Seton: American Saint* (Ithaca, NY: Cornell University Press, 2018).

That population grew exponentially in the nineteenth century as millions of immigrants poured in from Ireland, Germany, Italy, Poland, and other countries. Missionaries, including many consecrated women, were sent from Europe to tend to this population, as the number of people serving the Church in the United States was insufficient to meet the tremendous demand. We will encounter some of those missionaries, such as Saint Frances Xavier Cabrini, in the next chapter.

### The social witness of Catholic women in postrevolutionary Europe

While the Church thrived unexpectedly in the United States, she faced much uncertainty in Europe, as relationships between her leaders and the ruling elites of various countries kept shifting. Suppressions of religious communities, seizures of ecclesiastical properties, and waves of anti-Catholic persecution continued from the era of the Napoleonic Wars through the 1870s as more liberal and nationalistic revolutions played out.

In 1870, for example, the unification of the Italian peninsula was achieved and, to the shock of many, the Papal States were dissolved, ending a monarchical regime that had been in place for more than a thousand years. Popes had to pivot toward an entirely pastoral mode of governing the worldwide Church—something that was challenging as bishops, other clergy, and the laity and religious in many countries were sometimes cut off from direct communication with Rome and caught up in local political movements. In 1871, the archbishop of Paris, Georges Darboy, was murdered by leftist radicals who had taken over the French capital. Many Catholics in this period left for the shores of America from Germany, Switzerland, and other lands where secularistic,

liberal political efforts to co-opt Catholic schools and other
institutions forced them to make a choice between love of
God and loyalty to their homelands.

In the meantime, societies began changing dramatically
due to the Industrial Revolution that took off first in England
and the United States and then in Germany, Belgium, parts
of Italy and France, and other lands. While industrialization
created new economic opportunities for the rising middle and
laboring classes, it also caused suffering in rural and more traditional urban areas that were left behind, so to speak, by the
changing international economy.

Sometimes having to start from scratch after the devasta-
tions of the revolutionary period, Catholic women responded
creatively to such challenges. For example, two wealthy women
in the Italian city of Verona—Saint Magdalena di Canossa
and Blessed Leopoldina Naudet—worked to meet the needs
of the poor who suffered from aftershocks of the Napoleonic
invasions in the early nineteenth century. Canossa founded
the Canossian Daughters of Charity and a men's congregation that focused on the care of poor and sick people and paid
special attention to abandoned and delinquent young people.
Naudet, who founded the Sisters of the Holy Family, focused
on educating poor children in Verona—catechizing them
while encouraging their study of economics and English,
which was becoming a dominant business language. Her congregation also trained schoolteachers.

To the west in Turin (home to the holy shroud of Christ),
the French-born Juliette Colbert and her Italian husband, a
wealthy nobleman named Carlo Tancredi Falletti di Barolo,
assisted poor children, prisoners, unwed mothers, and victims
of child prostitution. They opened free schools and houses of
refuge and engaged in other personal ministries. Unable to
have children of their own, the couple worked with the local
archbishop to found the Sisters of Saint Anne, a congregation

devoted to nurturing neglected and suffering children, and they heroically assisted victims of cholera when an epidemic swept through the region. Sadly, Carlo died from this disease, leaving Juliette a widow in her early fifties. Sometime after this, Juliette—whose cause for canonization is open—became a Secular Franciscan and helped found another women's congregation, the Daughters of Jesus the Good Shepherd. She died in 1864, almost thirty years after her husband.

Switzerland also experienced much trauma in the era of the French Revolution, Napoleonic invasions, and liberal nation building. In some places, its sizable Catholic minority was swept up in an effort to resist the creation of a Swiss federal republic that was modeled to some degree on the young United States. In the years before the Swiss constitution was ratified in 1848, many Catholic monasteries were suppressed. Additionally, the Sonderbund War pitted some Catholic regions against the majority—consisting of liberals, Reformed Protestants, and many Catholics—who favored the federal project. Furthermore, the Jesuit order, which had been restored after a period of suppression by the papacy in 1814, was banished from the country.

In the Swiss canton of Fribourg, farming families that used traditional agricultural methods suffered new degrees of hardship due to economic shifts. Saint Marguerite Bays, a devout young seamstress in the town of Chavannes-les-Forts, assisted poor families by bringing them food and offering free laundry and sewing services. After becoming a Secular Franciscan, she also catechized poor children and tended to the sick. At one point, she became sick from bowel cancer but was miraculously healed on December 8, 1854, the day Pope Pius IX declared the dogma of the Blessed Mother's Immaculate Conception. After this, Marguerite began experiencing the stigmata and mystical encounters with Christ. She suffered from these experiences but did so silently, occupying herself with charitable projects until her death in 1879 at the age of sixty-three.

Women helped preserve and strengthen the Church in Switzerland in the middle and later decades of the nineteenth century, despite strong prejudices against Catholics who remained loyal to Rome at the time of the First Vatican Council and the dissolution of the Papal States. New Swiss congregations for women were even founded, such as the Sisters of the Holy Cross of Menzingen. Older congregations, such as the Capuchins, remained active in Switzerland, too.

A Swiss woman associated for a time with both these congregations was Saint María Bernarda Bütler, who lived from 1848 to 1924. Bütler was based in a Capuchin convent in the canton of St. Gallen when she was asked by a bishop in 1888 to cross the Atlantic to Ecuador to form a new congregation. She was forty years old at the time. In Ecuador, she founded the Franciscan Missionary Sisters of Mary Help of Sinners, which was devoted to poverty relief in that country. She and a group of sisters later moved on to Colombia, where she would spend the rest of her life. Her congregation later expanded to Brazil and Liechtenstein.

Postrevolutionary France was an especially fertile field for the efforts of Catholics to address social and spiritual problems. Exemplary are the stories of Saint Julie Billiart, Blessed Pauline Jaricot, and Amélie Soulacroix. Billiart, who lived through the revolution and knew the martyred Carmelites of Compiègne, risked her own life harboring a priest who refused to swear his loyalty to the revolutionary regime. She later founded the Sisters of Notre Dame de Namur. She and the sisters of this congregation were devoted to caring for and educating girls whose families had been displaced by the turmoil of the revolution.

Pauline Jaricot was born in the summer of 1799, a few months before Napoleon became the dictator of France.

Her family, based in the industrializing city of Lyons, were wealthy silk merchants with their own factory. From her late teen years onward, Pauline helped her father run the factory after her mother died. Her brother, in the meantime, pursued a priestly vocation—not something many Frenchmen did in that difficult time for the Church—and shared with Pauline news he heard about Catholic missions in China and America.

At a time when Frenchwomen had hardly any options for pursuing overseas mission work, Pauline began to assist missionaries in a creative way: by collecting small donations from workers in her father's factory. In 1822, along with some of the more enthusiastic laborers who contributed, she formed the Society for the Propagation of the Faith, an organization for assisting missionaries. This organization eventually developed into an international association that still exists as the oldest of four Pontifical Mission Societies headquartered in the Vatican.

Beyond all this, Jaricot, who became a Dominican tertiary and was directed spiritually by Saint John Vianney, founded the Association of the Living Rosary, which encouraged French people—many of whom had grown lax in the Catholic faith—to pray more and read more on spiritual themes. Furthermore, with money she inherited from her family, she bought a factory that produced blast furnaces (crucial for powering other industrializing factories) and set up housing next door for the workers and their families, to whom she also provided access to a nearby school and chapel. Her hope was to create a model Christian society, long before Pope Leo XIII—who issued the encyclical *Rerum Novarum* on the proper relationships that should exist among factory workers, managers, and owners—developed Catholic social teachings textually and pastorally.

Amélie Soulacroix, who lived from 1820 to 1894, was the wife of Blessed Frédéric Ozanam, the layman who founded the now worldwide Society of Saint Vincent de Paul, which promotes the holiness of the laity through dedicated service to the poor. As a young man, Ozanam was an outspoken journalist, favoring the papacy over a more nationalistic understanding of the Church that was popular among many French Catholic clergymen and theologians at the time. But he also felt challenged by critics who accused the Church of not doing enough for the poor. The Society of Saint Vincent de Paul was his response to this concern. Ozanam led it while also pursuing a career as a professor of literature in Paris and living an ordinary married life, which began for him in June 1841 when he married Soulacroix, whose father was a university official.

Soulacroix was a devoted wife, and she gave birth to a daughter, Marie, several years into their marriage. Tragically, the marriage was brought to an early end when Ozanam died of consumption in 1853 at only forty years of age. Already supportive of Ozanam's work with the Society of Saint Vincent de Paul and his promotion of Catholic principles as a writer and professor, Soulacroix spent the rest of her long life advancing her husband's work and pursuing other charitable projects and Catholic causes. For example, she assisted the missionary work of Cardinal Charles Lavigerie, who founded the Missionaries of Africa (nicknamed the *Pères Blancs* in French because of their white habits) in 1868. This congregation in time brought the Catholic faith to villages such as Ourous in Guinea, where today's Cardinal Robert Sarah grew up.

## Eugénie, the charitable empress of the French and early feminist

In the year prior to Frédéric Ozanam's death, the most powerful man in France—the newly declared Emperor Napoleon III, a nephew of the first Napoleon—was still a bachelor in his midforties and was searching for a wife and empress. Many French ladies were disappointed when he proposed to Eugénie de Montijo, a young woman of Spanish and Scottish heritage. Although Napoleon was a notorious womanizer, he was smitten with the virtuous and beautiful Eugénie, who would not submit to his advances before marriage. The two married in January 1853 inside Notre Dame Cathedral.

Eugénie suffered a miscarriage before giving birth to a son, Prince Louis-Napoléon. Her conjugal life after this was unhappy, as the emperor had numerous affairs. Eugénie abstained from relations with her husband throughout most of their marriage due to her disgust with his philandering and the diseases he brought home. But she was diligent in her duties as the empress and influenced French public life with her sincere and strong Catholic faith. She favored the Papal States against the revolutionaries in nearby Italy, and she sometimes tempered the liberal policies that her husband's governmental ministers favored.

Eugénie was devoted to charitable work. She patronized the Royal Hospital for the Blind, donated to struggling convents and monasteries, and worked closely with cholera patients during a great epidemic in the mid-1860s. When the Prussians invaded France in 1870, she converted the imperial palace, the Tuileries, into a war hospital. Eugénie furthermore established a foundation to assist poor French girls, and she promoted women's equality at a time when numerous women were entering France's industrializing labor force. Far ahead of her time, she favored granting the right to vote to French women, something that would not occur until 1944.

Napoleon III and Eugénie did not remain in power as long as expected. Their government, the French regime known as the Second Empire, was overthrown by new French revolutionaries in 1870, sending the emperor and empress into exile.

Despite the efforts of Catholic monarchists all over Europe, it was clear by this point—when the Papal States also fell and the bishops of the Church were gathered, in a spirit of alarm, at the First Vatican Council—that revolutionary liberalism was here to stay.

## Chapter 5

# The Era of Industrialization, Imperialism, and American Ascendancy

The nineteenth century saw the rise of four major industrial powers: Great Britain, the United States, a newly unified Germany, and France. Together with industrialization and unprecedented wealth creation in Europe and North America came a new era of Western empire building across the globe. Much of it was driven by a desire among liberal statesmen and industry captains to take advantage of the natural resources to be extracted from subordinated lands across the Americas, Asia, and Africa. Most famously, Great Britain—through a mix of violence, economic pressure, and negotiations—built a world empire "upon which the sun never sets". The French, too, especially under the Third Republic, built a large empire concentrated in West and North Africa and Southeast Asia.

The United States, while shying away from the language of "empire", also came to dominate the Western hemisphere and parts of East Asia, such as the Philippines, by the turn of the twentieth century. Indeed, the United States was in the position to become the world's greatest power by the 1910s, overtaking Britain in this role.

As a result of all this empire building, ordinary people around the world began experiencing changes that were for some traumatic, for others thrilling, and for many disorienting. Some suffered new degrees of poverty and marginalization, while others prospered as never before. At the same time, new technologies were developed, especially in the United States, that altered landscapes, the layouts of cities, the relationship of human beings to the natural world, and relationships among people. These included the locomotive, steamships, the telegraph, the electric light bulb, the typewriter, the telephone, photography, and the Gatling gun. Advances in pharmacy, medicine, surgery, and biological research changed expectations regarding the human life span. Meteorological discoveries made it easier to predict weather and natural disasters—a boon for industrializing, large-scale farms, ranches, and mining operations alike.

Many people began to view traditional religious beliefs as outmoded amid all this, believing that human beings no longer needed God or at least no longer needed to fear His judgments. Yet the Church, with her unchanging creed, remained constantly present in this changing world, responding to spiritual, emotional, bodily, and intellectual needs as she always had done. The Church also grew dramatically in this period, despite flagging fidelity among elites in once-Catholic lands. She grew exponentially in the United States, Africa, and Asia, and she remained the dominant religious presence in Latin American countries once ruled by Spain and Portugal.

The nineteenth-century Church's face was, furthermore, increasingly female due to the proliferation of new institutes of consecrated life for women, including congregations focused on missionary work, teaching, and health care. Indeed, by 1860, 60 percent of the Church's consecrated members were female, whereas women had made up only 40 percent eighty years earlier.[1] And, while some people rejected the Church's teachings, many others found new consolation and light in them, including some of those suffering the disorientation

---

[1]    Diarmaid MacCulloch, *Christianity: The First Three Thousand Years* (New York: Penguin, 2010), 819.

and marginalization that economic modernization, political liberalism, nationalism, and imperialism were causing.

## The Blessed Mother in a rapidly changing world

Historians of Catholicism note that the nineteenth century saw a marked increase in devotion to the Mother of Christ, which was spurred on by people claiming to see apparitions of her. Oxford University's Diarmaid MacCulloch, for example, writes, "The nineteenth century proved one of the most prolific periods for Mary's activity in the history of the Western Church since the twelfth century." He adds that in Europe and other parts of the world, Mary tended to appear "generally to women without money, education or power in remote locations, and often in association with the political upheavals or economic crises which repeatedly hit a society in the middle of dramatic transformations".[2]

Famous in this regard were the visions in Paris of young Saint Catherine Labouré. Newly professed with the Daughters of Charity, Labouré first saw Mary appear in July 1830, in the middle of the second French Revolution that toppled the Bourbon monarchy again after a period of royal restoration. Labouré received instructions from the Blessed Mother to promote a particular image of her that could be struck into medals for Catholics to wear. Because Mary was crowned with stars in Labouré's visions, the image used for the Miraculous Medal, as it came to be known, depicted her that way. The medals also bore the words, "O Mary, conceived without sin, pray for us who have recourse to thee."

By the 1840s, tens of millions of medals had been struck and Catholics all over France and beyond were drawing comfort

---

2  Ibid.

from them amid the uncertainties of the time, including further political unrest caused by economic changes and liberal,
nationalist movements that were increasingly anti-Catholic.

Among the many claims of Marian apparitions in the
nineteenth century, those that Church officials today deem
valid for devotion include Labouré's visions, as well as those
of several French children in the village of La Salette in 1846,
Saint Bernadette Soubirous' visions in Lourdes the following
decade, and those of a French farming family in the hamlet of
Pontmain in 1871. Likewise, the Church recognizes apparitions that took place in Wisconsin in 1859, the Polish village
of Gietrzwałd in 1877, and the Irish village of Knock in 1879.
The villagers in Gietrzwałd were suffering effects of imperial-
istic Germany's Kulturkampf—a political and cultural struggle that led to the banishment of priests and monastics who
refused to comply with new governmental directives that went
against their Catholic consciences.

The messages the visionaries heard from Our Lady often
concerned challenges the Church was facing in the period.
At La Salette, for example, the fourteen-year-old shepherd-
ess Mélanie Calvat and her eleven-year-old friend Maxi-
min Giraud reported that a weeping lady had appeared and
reproached French Catholics for working on Sundays, something their profit-hungry employers increasingly demanded.

Our Lady of Good Help, who appeared to a young Belgian
immigrant named Adele Brise near Green Bay, Wisconsin, in
1859, urged Brise to pray unceasingly for the conversion of
sinners and to gather up children in frontier places "and teach
them what they should know for salvation".[3] Brise became a
schoolteacher and began to instruct children in various homes
and eventually in a schoolhouse. Becoming a Franciscan

---

3    Michael J. Pfeifer, *The Making of American Catholicism: Regional Culture and the Catholic
Experience* (New York: New York University Press, 2020), 80.

tertiary, Brise, along with other women who took up similar work, helped sow the seeds of Catholic faith and culture in a region that welcomed more and more immigrant families each year but lacked developed, well-staffed Catholic institutions to efficiently meet their needs.

Even before some of the most famous Marian apparitions of the period, Pope Pius IX saw a need to promote devotion to the Mother of God in the modernizing world. He proclaimed the dogma of the Immaculate Conception—that Mary was conceived by Saint Anne without the stain of Original Sin, by the merits of her future Son, Jesus—on December 8, 1854. Although popular devotion to the Immaculate Conception had existed long before this, it increased after December 8 was made a holy day honoring Mary's special character. Within a few years, it was strongly reinforced by one Marian apparition in particular: in a sleepy market town in the Pyrenees region of southern France.

### Bernadette of Lourdes, one of the first celebrity saints

The dogma of the Immaculate Conception became better known and appreciated than the pope was able to achieve on his own after a barely literate peasant girl experienced miraculous apparitions of a lady who referred to herself as the Immaculate Conception. That girl was Saint Bernadette Soubirous.

Born in 1844 in the small town of Lourdes in southern France, Bernadette was the daughter of François Soubirous, a humble miller, and Louise Casterot, a laundress. Bernadette was the eldest of the couple's eventual nine children.

The close-knit Soubirous family enjoyed a decent life until hard economic times hit France after the Revolution of 1848 that led to Napoleon III's coming to power. By the time Bernadette was a teenager, she and her family were impoverished and she suffered from asthma and other health problems they could not afford to treat.

At fourteen, Bernadette was still largely illiterate, had difficulty remembering her catechism lessons, and as a result had not yet been permitted to receive her First Holy Communion. Although it was not unusual at the time for young people to receive First Communion as teenagers, Bernadette determined to overcome her learning problems and finally received the Body of Christ in June 1858.

Not long after this, while gathering firewood near a grotto close to her family's home, Bernadette heard a sound like a gust of wind and then noticed an unusual light and a female form. She told a priest what she had seen and was later questioned by a local commissioner who worked for the French government. He accused her of claiming to see the Blessed Virgin, but she denied she had said any such thing.

In the coming days, Bernadette returned to the grotto and saw the same presence more clearly. It was a young lady dressed in white with a blue sash, and she had golden roses at her feet. The lady, whom no one else could see or hear, said, "I am the Immaculate Conception." She urged Bernadette to pray and do penance for the conversion of sinners, as well as to drink from a spring of water that began flowing from the rocks she was standing on. The lady also asked that a chapel be built at the site.

Bernadette reported everything she had seen and heard to local authorities. Some were moved by her sincerity and believed her. Others, including the local bishop, thought she was hallucinating. Journalists and other curious people began flocking to Lourdes to watch Bernadette at the times she expected to see the lady. Many people mocked Bernadette and even trampled on roses that pilgrims left near the grotto. Other visitors, hoping to be healed of ailments and disabilities, found that the spring of water had healing powers.

By Bernadette's time, newspapers were common, so her visions sparked a mid-nineteenth-century version of a media frenzy. As Bernadette became a celebrity, all sorts of temptations came her way, including offers of money and requests to bless rosaries and other objects. Yet she insisted on staying poor and refused to bless anything. She wanted the Blessed Mother alone—and her messages about prayer, repentance, and God's love for all sinners and suffering people—to be the focus.

The public attention and scrutiny proved too much for Bernadette. She decided to enter the convent of the Sisters of Charity and Christian Instruction at Nevers. She took the religious name Sister Marie-Bernard and was able to devote herself to prayer and taking care of the sick who came to the sisters for help. Her prayers focused on the redemption of sinners, as the Blessed Mother had requested.

Bernadette suffered poor health and was bedridden by her early thirties. Unable to sleep many nights, she offered herself continuously as a sacrifice, united to Christ Crucified. In this period, however, she received visitors, including bishops, at the convent, and she was also in touch with various people through letters, including Pope Pius IX, to whom she said at one point, "My weapons are prayer and sacrifice, and I shall pray and sacrifice until my last breath."[4]

Bernadette died at age thirty-five on April 16, 1879. By the time of her death, the grotto at Lourdes had become a major pilgrimage site. In time, a great basilica, consecrated to Our Lady of the Rosary in 1901, would stand there. Eight years later, in 1909, Bernadette's body was exhumed and discovered to be incorrupt.

Today, Lourdes is the most visited Christian shrine in the world. Many miracles have been reported among those

---

4    St. Bernadette of Lourdes to Pope Leo XIII, December 17, 1876, in Patricia A. McEachern, ed., *A Holy Life: The Writings of St. Bernadette* (San Francisco: Ignatius Press, 2005), 173.

seeking healing from the waters there. Although she sought escape from fame, Bernadette was canonized on the Feast of the Immaculate Conception in 1933. She is the patron saint of Lourdes, shepherds and shepherdesses, those suffering bodily illnesses, those suffering poverty, and those ridiculed for their faith.

### Thérèse of Lisieux and the Little Way that changed the world

Another popular French shrine sits more than five hundred miles due north of Lourdes. It is dedicated to Saint Thérèse of Lisieux, another nineteenth-century nun who died young. She was a Discalced Carmelite, like the martyrs of Compiègne and Teresa of Avila.

Marie-Françoise-Thérèse Martin was born in the industrialized city of Alençon on January 2, 1873. Her parents—also canonized saints—were Louis Martin and Zélie Guérin Martin. Both her parents had wished to enter religious life when young but were rejected by the orders to which they applied, an experience over which they bonded when courting. Once married, they worked together in the profitable business of lacemaking. Creating a genteel home out of their earnings, the two went on to have nine children, only five of whom— all daughters—survived infancy. All five would become nuns.

Thérèse, the youngest, was only four when her mother died in 1877. Her father then took over the upbringing of the children, so Thérèse grew up especially close to him. Louis wanted his children to spend time with people who had known their mother, so he relocated his family further north to the town of Lisieux where some of Zélie's relatives lived.

Later, in her autobiography, *Story of a Soul*, Thérèse described how her mother's death affected her: "I . . . became timid and retiring, sensitive to an excessive degree. One look was enough to reduce me to tears, and the only way I was content was to be left alone completely."[5]

Thérèse also became unusually focused on God as a child. One of her most famous reflections about how God relates to all of us—one that gave her the nickname "The Little Flower"—stems from a realization she had while quite young, around the time her mother died. Flower gardens were an ordinary sight where she lived, and in thinking about the different flowers she was becoming familiar with, God taught her "this mystery":

> I understood how all the flowers He has created are beautiful, how the splendor of the rose and the whiteness of the Lily do not take away the perfume of the little violet or the delightful simplicity of the daisy. I understood that if all flowers wanted to be roses, nature would lose her springtime beauty....
>
> And so it is in the world of souls, Jesus' garden. He willed to create great souls comparable to lilies and roses, but He has created smaller ones and these must be content to be daisies or violets destined to give joy to God's glances when He looks down at His feet. Perfection consists ... in being what He wills us to be.[6]

Thérèse's spiritual precociousness was encouraged by two childhood experiences. At age ten, she was healed from a serious illness after many prayers were offered for her to Our Lady of Victories. Then, at age eleven, while being educated about the faith by Benedictine nuns, she had a profound experience of union with Christ. This was shortly before she received First Holy Communion. (Eleven was exceptionally young for

---

5   John Clarke, O.C.D., trans., *Story of a Soul: The Autobiography of Saint Thérèse of Lisieux*, 3rd ed. (Washington, DC: ICS Publications, 1996), 34–35.
6   Ibid., 14.

receiving First Communion at that time; it was not until 1910 that Pope Pius X decreed that children could start receiving at age seven.)

Another reason Thérèse became so devout was that two of her sisters, Pauline and Marie, had entered a Carmelite community nearby in Lisieux. Thérèse wished to follow them into the convent, but since the sixteenth century, girls younger than sixteen could not enter religious life.

Thérèse refused to accept this law of the Church without a fight. While visiting Italy with her father on a pilgrimage, Thérèse begged Pope Leo XIII—after her group had been granted a general audience with him—to let her enter the convent in Lisieux at age fifteen. The pope was alarmed by the intensity of the young girl, who grabbed him around the knees when his attendants attempted to pull her away from him. But Thérèse got her way. On April 9, 1888, a few months after her fifteenth birthday, Thérèse entered the convent in Lisieux. She received a Carmelite habit early the following year and professed solemn vows—of poverty, chastity, and obedience—on September 8, 1890.

In *Story of a Soul*, Thérèse shared how her understanding of the Carmelite vocation developed before becoming a nun. She had readily understood why the Discalced Carmelites were dedicated to praying for souls in general, but it took her experience as a pilgrim to understand why Teresa of Avila had ordered her sisters to pray specifically for priests. In Rome, Thérèse observed that even the best priests are fragile and need constant prayers: "I learned that, though their dignity raises them above the angels, they are nevertheless weak and fragile men. If *holy priests* ... show in their conduct their extreme need for prayers, what is to be said of those who are tepid?"[7]

---

In the convent, Thérèse—now Thérèse of the Child Jesus—faced many small and large challenges of her own in pursuing the life of Christian perfection. An especially difficult period came in the summer of 1894 when she was twenty-one. Her father died, and this tested her faith.

Thérèse persevered through this darkness, however, as she developed a spiritual approach called "the Little Way of Spiritual Childhood", something she taught to younger novices in the community. She also had a missionary spirit and decided to unite herself spiritually to missionaries overseas in places such as West Africa and Vietnam. She even corresponded with some of them.

Another key moment in Thérèse's journey occurred on June 9, 1895, the Solemnity of the Most Holy Trinity. Twenty-two at the time, she offered herself sacrificially to God's merciful love. And she began writing her autobiography at the request of her religious superior, who was also her biological sister Pauline.

Some months later, late in the night on Holy Thursday in 1896, Thérèse suffered a dry, bloody cough, which was the first sign of tuberculosis, the disease that would kill her. She welcomed this event as a mysterious visitation of her spouse, Jesus, but also entered a trial of faith that would last until her death. As her health declined and her spiritual trials continued, she continued to write, borne up by grace and motivated by the insights that kept coming to her during her hours of reflection and prayer.

Thérèse was eventually transferred to the infirmary of her convent. Her sisters, biological and spiritual, collected her sayings and writings. Her suffering only intensified, but she accepted it with heroic patience up to the moment of her death at age twenty-four on September 30, 1897. Her final words, on her deathbed, were "My God ... I love you!" Not long before this, Thérèse had written to a missionary priest with whom she corresponded, "I am not dying, I am entering into life."[8]

Thérèse was canonized in 1925. Pope Pius XI also proclaimed her Universal Patroness of the Missions, alongside the Jesuit saint Francis Xavier. During World War II, Pope Pius XII named her co-patroness of France with Joan of Arc, a saint who had only recently been canonized herself and one whose canonization Thérèse had advocated while she was alive. And in 1997, Pope John Paul II declared her to be a Doctor of the Church—the youngest person, and only the third woman at the time, to be so honored.

The teachings in *Story of a Soul,* which was published shortly after Thérèse's death, were what convinced the most powerful and educated leaders of the Church to elevate the young Carmelite in these ways. One passage in particular demonstrates her profound understanding of God's infinitely loving nature in relation to His finite creatures who yearn to be freed from creaturely limits:

> To be Your spouse, to be a Carmelite, and by my union with You to be the mother of souls, should not this suffice me? And yet it is not so.... I feel the vocation of the Warrior ... the Apostle, the Doctor, the Martyr.... I feel within my soul the courage of the Crusader, the Papal Guard....
>
> I feel in me the vocation of the Priest....
>
> I would like to enlighten souls as did the Prophets and the Doctors. I would like to travel over the whole earth to preach Your Name and to plant Your glorious Cross on infidel soil. But ... one mission alone would not be sufficient.... I would want to preach the Gospel on all the five continents simultaneously.... I would be a missionary ... from the beginning of creation until the consummation of the ages....

---

8    Ibid., 271.

[Such] desires caused me a veritable martyrdom....

Charity gave me the key to my vocation.... I understood that the Church had a Heart and that this Heart was burning with love. I understood it was Love alone that made the Church's members act, that if Love ever became extinct, apostles would not preach the Gospel and martyrs would not shed their blood. I understood that Love comprised all vocations, that Love was everything, that it embraced all times and places ... in a word, that it was eternal!

Then, in the excess of my delirious joy, I cried out: O Jesus, my Love ... my vocation, at last I have found it ... my vocation is Love!

Yes, I have found my place in the Church and it is You, O my God. who have given me this place; in the heart of the Church, my Mother, I shall be Love.[9]

Because of passages like this, *Story of a Soul*, in time, surpassed Augustine's *Confessions*, Teresa of Avila's autobiography, and Francis de Sales' *Introduction to the Devout Life* as the most widely read work of Catholic spirituality in the world.

### Frances Xavier Cabrini and the missionary vocation of women

Around the time young Thérèse of Lisieux was first wishing to be a missionary, a young Italian woman, Saint Frances Xavier Cabrini, was attempting to establish a new institute called the Missionary Sisters of the Sacred Heart of Jesus based in the Lombardy region of the newly unified Kingdom of Italy. But Cabrini faced opposition in high levels of the Church. Although women had served in mission settings for centuries, some churchmen in the late nineteenth century

---

9   Ibid., 192–94.

still saw evangelistic missions solely as men's work. Thus, Cabrini found herself arguing to one of them, "If the mission of announcing the Lord's Resurrection to His Apostles had been entrusted to Mary Magdalene, it would seem a very good thing to confide to other women an evangelizing mission."[10]

Fortunately for Cabrini, a churchman who liked what she was doing was Pope Leo XIII. In 1888, Leo blessed her institute, which was already running several orphanages and schools in Italy. The following year, he surprised the thirty-eight-year-old foundress, who was hoping he would send her to China, by saying, "Not to the East, but to the West." The pope sent the disappointed but obedient Mother Cabrini to New York City. There, she and her Missionary Sisters taught the Catholic faith and brought Christ's charity to an exploding population of poor Italian immigrants.[11]

Mother Cabrini went on to found numerous convents, orphanages, schools, nurseries, and hospitals in the northeastern United States, Illinois, Colorado, Washington, California, multiple Latin American countries, and Europe, where she returned several times by steamship, despite her chronic fear of boat travel.

The United States was still considered mission territory by the Vatican when Cabrini first crossed the Atlantic. In 1908, Pope Pius X lifted that designation, given the maturing state of the Church in the country. That was less than a decade before Cabrini died at age sixty-seven. By the time she was canonized in 1946, the Missionary Sisters were laboring in China, where Cabrini had once dreamed of going herself.

Although Cabrini had not initially wished to go to America, the connections she made as a prominent foundress in

---

10   Quoted in Mary Louise Sullivan, M.S.C., *Mother Cabrini: "Italian Immigrant of the Century"* (New York: Center for Migration Studies, 1992), 36.

11   Philippa Provenzano, M.S.C., trans., *To the Ends of the Earth: The Missionary Travels of Frances X. Cabrini* (New York: Center of Migration Studies, 2001), xvi–xvii.

New York City—already a commercial and cultural capital of the world—were crucial to the expansion of her ministries across several continents. The young American Church was becoming missionary in its own right by the turn of the twentieth century, partly because the United States was becoming a major presence globally.

Because the forms of consecrated life open to Catholic women had expanded so much by the nineteenth century, there were more opportunities than ever before for women to serve as missionaries—if not always with that title—in lands where Christianity was still being introduced. Ironically, many of those opportunities emerged in connection with the expansion of the secularized, postrevolutionary French state and the expansion of Great Britain and the United States, both of which were culturally dominated by Protestantism.

### Pioneering women missionaries of the nineteenth century

Several pioneering women missionaries were Frenchwomen who labored in parts of Africa where the modern French state launched aggressive new colonial efforts. One of them was Blessed Anne-Marie Javouhey, who lived from 1779 to 1851. After she and her three biological sisters started several schools and an orphanage for poor children close to their home village of Jallanges in eastern France, she founded the Sisters of Saint Joseph of Cluny in 1807.

In 1817, Javouhey was asked by French officials to open a school on Réunion Island, a French colony east of Madagascar. She and other sisters of her congregation also began missionary work in hospitals in French Sénégal in West Africa. After learning of her work, British colonial officials invited her congregation to care for victims of an epidemic in Gambia and other suffering people in Sierra Leone.

Javouhey also crossed the Atlantic to French Guiana. There, she and more than thirty of her sisters founded a settlement called Mana, where they helped black people just emancipated from slavery transition into a new life of freedom. This won Javouhey enemies, who almost killed her. Later in life, she faced opposition from Church authorities in France, where she spent her final years engaged in work such as caring for the wounded during the Revolution of 1848.[12]

A contemporary of Javouhey, Saint Émilie de Vialar, lived from 1797 to 1856. She founded the Sisters of Saint Joseph of the Apparition, who became active in Algeria because of a family connection she had to colonial authorities there after the French invasion of 1830. With her own money, Vialar opened a hospital in Boufarik near Algiers, where a cholera outbreak was ravaging the population.

Vialar and seventeen other Sisters of Saint Joseph expanded their ministries in Algeria, focusing on care of the poor and the sick. This won them the approval of some Muslim women in the region. The Catholic bishop in Algiers, however, wanted the women to focus more directly on catechesis and attempted to assert jurisdiction over them when Vialar insisted they were under the authority of another bishop in France. These tensions interrupted the women's work in Algeria, but they went on to establish hospitals and schools elsewhere in North Africa and the Middle East.[13]

Vialar and Javouhey established a precedent for more women to serve as missionaries in different parts of the world. And while some churchmen in the era objected to female missionary activity, others were actively recruiting women into mission work even before Mother Cabrini's time. We see this in the examples of Blessed Maria Caterina Troiani and Maria

---

12  Sarah A. Curtis, *Civilizing Habits: Women Missionaries and the Revival of French Empire* (New York: Oxford University Press, 2010), 177–262.
13  Ibid., 101–74.

Giuseppa Scandola, who served as missionaries in Egypt and Sudan, respectively.

Troiani, who grew up in the Papal States before Italy's revolutionary unification, was a Franciscan nun who answered a call by a bishop, Perpetuo Guasco da Solero, to join a new Franciscan missionary institute in Cairo, which was then under Ottoman rule. By 1859, when she was in her midforties, Troiani and a group of other Franciscan women were in Egypt, focusing on educating poor girls, equipping them with practical skills for employment, and instructing them in the teachings of the Church. They called their institute the Franciscan Missionary Sisters of Egypt, and their congregation is still active today as the Franciscan Missionary Sisters of the Immaculate Heart of Mary. Troiani spent the rest of her life in Egypt, dying at age seventy-four.

A generation younger than Troiani, Scandola would not live so long. Born in 1849 in then Austrian-ruled Verona, Scandola was in her early twenties when she met a missionary priest, Saint Daniele Comboni, who was eventually made a bishop. While home in Europe after having done some missionary work in Central Africa, Comboni was eager to recruit women into this mission context, as they would have better access to the women of tribal societies that practiced Islam and maintained strict gender divisions.

Scandola volunteered, becoming the second woman to join Comboni's new institute, the Missionary Sisters of Verona. Professing vows at twenty-eight, Scandola left for Sudan, south of Egypt, which was partly under British rule. She spent more than twenty-five years laboring as a missionary among diverse communities in the region. Then, at fifty-four, she traveled to a place called Lul along the White Nile, where she began learning the local Shilluk language so that she could communicate about Christianity to the local people. However, on September 1, 1903, she offered her life in exchange for a priest who had been taken prisoner. She was killed in his place. Her cause for beatification is currently open in Rome.

In more settled colonial contexts, Catholic women proved to be effective administrators and staff of charitable hospitals, schools, and orphanages. For this reason, authorities even in the British imperial establishment were often happy to welcome them to their colonies, seeing the social and cultural benefits of their presence as outweighing the "problem" that they were also determined to spread Catholicism among indigenous populations. Thus, by the end of the nineteenth century, female Catholic missionaries were found in places such as British-colonial South Africa and India.

Among them was a French-born sister who took the name Mary of the Passion after she was sent by her superiors in the Sisters of Mary Reparatrix to serve in the city of Madurai in British-controlled India. Mary of the Passion, who lived from 1839 to 1904, in time secured permission from Pope Pius IX to form her own institute, the Missionaries of Mary, who were an important precedent for Mother Cabrini's institute. Devoted to both contemplative prayer and providing medical care to the poor, the Missionaries of Mary had eighty-six communities operating by the end of their foundress's life, not only in India, but also in China and other countries across the increasingly interconnected modern globe.

### Josephine Bakhita and the globalizing prewar Church

As the Church continued to grow in lands where Christianity was being introduced, conversions still happened in the secularizing lands which had once been the heart of Christendom. One was sealed with the sacrament of baptism in 1890 in the war-torn, newly unified nation-state of Italy. The woman who had requested the sacrament was Josephine Bakhita, who came from the Islamic Sultanate of Darfur in what is today Sudan. Bakhita went on to become a religious sister, affecting those who knew her with her piety, kindness, and love to such an extent that her cause for sainthood was pursued. In 2000, she was declared to be the first Sudanese saint and the patron saint of her homeland.

Bakhita, whose path to Italy and the Church was full of agonies, was born in 1869 in the small village of Olgossa in Darfur. Bakhita was not the name her parents gave her, but her birth name is lost to history. Her people, the Daju, were powerful in the region and were occupied with farming and hunting. They practiced Islam and some traditional religious customs that predated Islam's introduction centuries before. As was true in many African states in the mid-nineteenth century, there was an active slave trade in the region linked to markets in the Ottoman Empire. And, tragically, Bakhita was kidnapped at the age of nine by slavers and transported to the city of El Obeid, a Sudanese city with ties to Ottoman Egypt. Her captors renamed her Bakhita, which stems from the Arabic word for "lucky".[14]

Bakhita was sold several times to different vicious masters. She suffered beatings, cutting, branding, and other cruelties. One of her owners cut her skin numerous times and poured salt on her wounds, permanently scarring her. Her life changed, however, after she was purchased by the Italian consul at Khartoum, Callisto Legnani. He took her to Italy to serve a family friend as a nanny but chose not to inform her that under Italian law she would legally be freed from slavery.

Once in Italy, Bakhita served as a slave in the household of Augusto Michieli in a suburb of Venice and was soon sent

---

14   Roberto Italo Zanini, *Bakhita: From Slave to Saint*, trans. Andrew Matt (San Francisco: Ignatius Press, 2013), Kindle.

into Venice itself to serve Michieli's daughter, Mimmina. Mimmina was enrolled in a school for girls run by the Canossian Daughters of Charity, who by this point operated many schools, hospitals, and other ministries in Europe and Asia. Bakhita was attracted to the Canossians' way of life, and she learned about the Catholic faith from a sister named Maria Fabretti. It was due to Fabretti's influence that Bakhita, twenty-one at the time, accepted baptism in 1890, taking the Christian name Josephine Margaret.[15]

Around this same time, after Mimmina's father attempted to force her to return to Sudan with the family when he was given an assignment there, Bakhita finally learned of the Italian law against slavery, which meant that she could not be treated as a slave by the Michielis. She found recourse in the Italian court system. With the support of the Canossian sisters and Cardinal Domenico Agostini, the patriarch of Venice, Bakhita received a formal judgment that she had been free the entire time she had been in Italy.

In 1893, the Canossians welcomed Bakhita as a novice. Within three years, she professed vows and was sent to Schio, northwest of Venice, where she resided as a member of the Canossian community for more than four decades. Struck by her kindness, charisma, and sanctity, the Canossians published her life story in 1931. Bakhita died in Schio on February 8, 1947, after having witnessed the ravages of two world wars. Thousands of people paid their respects, and her cause for canonization opened quickly thereafter.

Bakhita prayed often for the young and growing Church throughout Africa, even though she never returned to the continent. Her story, including the ways it was shared internationally before and after her death, demonstrates how globally interconnected the Church had become by her lifetime.

---

15   Ibid.

## Mary Ledóchowska, Polish aristocrat
## devoted to the Church in Africa

The same is true of the story of a contemporary of Bakhita's, Blessed Mary Theresa Ledóchowska, a Polish noblewoman who devoted decades of her life to the young Church in Africa. Ledóchowska lived from 1862 to 1922.

In her early thirties, Ledóchowska founded the Missionary Sisters of Saint Peter Claver. This was in 1894, some years after she had become both a Franciscan tertiary and a lady-in-waiting to Princess Alice of Bourbon-Parma, a grand duchess of the Austro-Hungarian Empire. While in royal service, she encountered some missionary sisters who were raising money for people suffering from leprosy far away in Madagascar. She also learned of an international campaign against slavery, which was still practiced in some African countries. Ledóchowska established committees throughout the Austro-Hungarian Empire that promoted the antislavery cause and raised awareness about women's mistreatment in some African societies. She also wrote a novel, *Zaida*, that did the same, and she started a column in a German-language journal that conveyed news from missionaries working throughout Africa.

Ledóchowska's column developed into a magazine titled *Echo aus Afrika* that first appeared in 1889. It is still published today by the Claverian sisters. The Polish noblewoman's role as the founding publisher of a successful magazine with an international readership was remarkable for a woman of that time.

By 1894, Ledóchowska had Pope Leo XIII's blessing to recruit more Claverian sisters, who had chosen as their patron Saint Peter Claver, a Spanish Jesuit missionary priest of the seventeenth century who had worked among enslaved Africans in Latin America and who had just been canonized in 1888, the same year Ledóchowska's brother Wlodomir was finishing his studies at the Jesuits' Pontifical Gregorian University in Rome. Wlodomir would go on to become the superior general of the whole Society of Jesus, taking inspiration from his sister's work into his leadership of the world's most famous missionary order.

Ledóchowska and the first Claverian sisters were devoted primarily to raising awareness in Europe of the extent, struggles, and hopes of the Church in Africa. They raised funds and provided other support for diverse missionary communities across the continent and supplied them with Bibles, hymnals, and dictionaries. In time, sisters of the congregation would go to African countries as missionaries, though their foundress never left Europe. Beatified in 1975 by Pope Paul VI, Ledóchowska had emphasized long before the fathers at Vatican II that all baptized Christians are called to be missionaries in some way. She also taught numerous laypeople, consecrated people, and clergymen alike the importance of spiritual communion with all the baptized across the globe.

### Marianne Cope, German American missionary to Hawaii

Another woman of the nineteenth-century Church was already teaching something similar in her adopted home of Hawaii when Ledóchowska was first learning about the Church in Africa. This was Saint Marianne Cope, who lived from 1838 to 1918.

Cope, whose given name was Barbara Koob, was one of ten children born into a farming family in the Grand Duchy of Hesse (today western Germany). In 1839, while Barbara was still a baby, the Koobs immigrated to the United States and changed their surname to Cope, which in their new English-speaking environment was a more phonetic spelling of the German name Koob.

Growing up in Utica, New York, Cope was raised with a strong Catholic faith and desired to become a nun. She worked in a factory for a time, however, before joining the Sisters of Saint Francis in Syracuse, New York, at age twenty-four. This Franciscan congregation was founded in Philadelphia by a Bavarian immigrant and widow named Maria Anna Boll, with the help of Saint John Neumann. It was initially devoted to educating German immigrant children.

Taking the religious name Marianne, Cope eventually, at thirty-one, became a nurse and administrator at Saint Joseph's Hospital in Syracuse, which was one of several hospitals staffed by the Sisters of Saint Francis. Her approach was controversial, as she would welcome alcoholics and other people considered to be undeserving of charity into the hospital. This, however, did not stop Cope from being selected for the post of provincial mother of her congregation.

Sometime after this, in 1883, Cope received an invitation from a priest friend to travel to the then-independent Kingdom of Hawaii in the Pacific Ocean to care for leprosy patients and to assist in the management of schools and hospitals. She accepted, writing back, "I am hungry for the work.... I am not afraid of any disease."[16]

Cope and six other sisters arrived in Honolulu in November 1883. They took over the Kaka'ako Branch Hospital on the island of Oahu, where those suffering from leprosy (Hansen's disease) came in large numbers. Within two years, they established a home for the healthy daughters of patients suffering from the disease.

When Cope arrived in Hawaii, a Belgian priest named Damien de Veuster—later remembered as Saint Damien of Molokai—had been working among those suffering from

---

16  Quoted in Cardinal José Saraiva Martins, "Bl. Marianne Cope (1838–1918): Virgin, Professed Sister of St Francis, Missionary to Leprosy Patients", May 14, 2005, www.vatican.va/news_services/liturgy/saints/ns_lit_doc_20050514_molokai_en.html.

leprosy on the island of Molokai for about a decade. The two future saints met in January 1884. In 1886, after Father Damien contracted the then-incurable disease, Cope welcomed him into her hospital, while other Catholics in Honolulu treated him as an outcast.

Eventually, Cope and several sisters relocated to Molokai, where they tended to Father Damien in his last days. They assured him that they would carry on his work. After his death in 1889, Cope oversaw the expansion of her sisters' ministries among leprosy patients and their family members. She devoted the rest of her life to this work. She died at age eighty on August 9, 1918, never having caught leprosy and never having returned home to Syracuse.


### Katharine Drexel, American heiress devoted to black and native education

At the time that young Marianne Cope was beginning her novitiate, the United States was in the middle of its terrible Civil War, which resulted in the death of some 620,000 soldiers and another 50,000 civilians. This war brought an end to legalized slavery in the United States, a system that had oppressed black people of African ancestry since long before the United States was founded. Even many years after the war, prejudices prevailed throughout the nation regarding the ways in which people of different colors could mingle socially or work as equals.

Such prejudices were strong in Pennsylvania's largest city of Philadelphia when a young heiress there named Katharine Mary Drexel was discerning what God wanted her to do with her life. Born on November 26, 1858, she was the second daughter of a wealthy Catholic investor, Francis Anthony Drexel, and his Protestant wife, Hannah Langstroth. Her sister, three years older, was named Elizabeth.

The young family soon suffered the tragedy of Hannah's early death. Francis remarried quickly, and his second wife, Emma Bouvier, became a mother to Katharine and Elizabeth and gave them another sister, Louise. Emma modeled to all three girls something that would shape their lives: she was devoutly Catholic and committed to serving the poor with the wealth she enjoyed. Until her own early death when Katharine was fourteen, she would distribute alms to the poor out of the Drexels' grand home on Philadelphia's Walnut Street.[17]

When Katharine was sixteen, her father died, leaving her and her sisters large inheritances. The girls shared, in trust, a third of Francis Drexel's fifteen-million-dollar estate, which was a staggering fortune in that era. All three sisters went on to use their shares for charitable purposes: Elizabeth and Louise, who both later married, established the Saint Francis Industrial School for Boys northeast of Philadelphia. Louise went on to become a great American Catholic philanthropist.

Katharine, however, became the most famous sister. In her early thirties, after completing a novitiate with the Sisters of Mercy in Pittsburgh, Katharine in 1891 formed a new congregation for women devoted to the education of poor Native American and African American children. She did so at the urging of a friend, the Jesuit priest James O'Connor, who was the first bishop of Omaha, Nebraska. She named the congregation the Sisters of the Blessed Sacrament for Indians and Colored People and established its motherhouse in Cornwells Heights, northeast of Philadelphia. She became the congregation's first superior and had twelve women under her authority by 1892.

Prior to this, Drexel had generously funded a new Sunday school for black children on Pine Street in Philadelphia. This institution grew into the parish of Saint Peter Claver, the first

---

17  Cheryl C.D. Hughes, *Katharine Drexel: The Riches-to-Rags Story of an American Catholic Saint* (Grand Rapids, MI: Eerdmans, 2014), 18.

African American Catholic parish in the Archdiocese of Philadelphia. By 1892, a boarding school for black children was operating next door to the sisters' motherhouse.

Drexel's decision to become a consecrated sister and devote herself to serving people of color sent shock waves through high society, as Drexel had been a highly eligible heiress and had received marriage proposals. In time, however, she would become less famous for rejecting a life of privilege than for the impact she and the Sisters of the Blessed Sacrament had on numerous young black and Native American people in Pennsylvania and other states.

Drexel and the sisters' most well-known project was the establishment of a high school in New Orleans that grew, by 1925, into Xavier University of Louisiana, the first Catholic institution of higher learning for black students. Though they faced great opposition when developing this university, by 1928 the Sisters of the Blessed Sacrament were awarding their first degrees to black women and men, lay and religious, with the approval of the Louisiana Department of Education.[18]

By the time Drexel died on March 3, 1955, at the age of ninety-six, the Sisters of the Blessed Sacrament had more than five hundred members. Ironically, they had been welcoming women of color among their own ranks for only about six years. This was not, however, due to a lack of interest among black women.

### Pioneering African American consecrated women

When the Sisters of the Blessed Sacrament were first launching their ministries, a woman of African and Native American ancestry from New Orleans, Mother Mathilda Beasley,

---

18  Shannen Dee Williams, *Subversive Habits: Black Catholic Nuns in the Long African American Freedom Struggle* (Durham, NC: Duke University Press, 2022), 86.

attempted to join forces with them after forming her own institute for African American women. Beasley had been born into slavery and had converted to Catholicism in 1869 before marrying a man who later died young. As a widow of means, Beasley in 1887 established a refuge for black girls in Savannah, Georgia, called the Saint Francis Home for Colored Orphans. Two years later, she formed the Sisters of the Third Order of Saint Francis, who ran a school for girls too.

After Beasley's ministries began to struggle financially, the bishop of Savannah, Thomas Becker, attempted to convince Mother Katharine Mary Drexel to incorporate Beasley's congregation into the Sisters of the Blessed Sacrament. It was at that point, in 1893, that Drexel's congregation decided formally to exclude women of color from their ranks—something enforced for almost sixty years.[19]

Beasley's congregation worked out, instead, an informal relationship with another Catholic women's congregation, the Missionary Franciscan Sisters of the Immaculate Conception, who were devoted to educating black children whose parents had been slaves. Sadly, Beasley's congregation did not survive long after its foundress's death in 1901.

Beasley's Sisters of the Third Order of Saint Francis was the sixth congregation established for black women in the United States. The congregation owed much to the earlier example of Mother Mary Elizabeth Lange, who died in 1882 at age ninety-seven. Born around the year 1784 in the city of Santiago in Spanish Cuba, Lange was the daughter of a woman of African and Jewish ancestry and a man who had been a slave in the French colony of Saint-Domingue (what became Haiti). Given the name Elizabeth Clarisse, Lange did not grow up in slavery but received a decent education for a girl in the colonial-era Caribbean. She immigrated to the United States in her twenties, settling in Baltimore in 1813.

---

19  Ibid., 55–56.

Lange started a school for black children in her home in Baltimore's Fell's Point neighborhood. Working with a French-born Sulpician priest and several other women of African ancestry, she formed the Oblate Sisters of Providence, a community that received formal approval from the archbishop of Baltimore in 1829 and from Rome in late 1831. This was after Lange and her associates had not been permitted admission into any existing Catholic congregations due to their race. Her congregation was the first for black women in the world. Lange served as the Oblates' superior general from 1829 to 1832 and again from 1834 to 1842.[20]

Lange and the Oblate Sisters of Providence faced many challenges, including from churchmen who attempted to suppress their institute or at least make sure they served only in servile capacities instead of running a school for black children. This was at a time when slavery was still legal in Maryland and other southern states.

Ironically, slavery was a cause of the growth of black Catholic populations, which required more attention and care from the Church than most Catholic leaders then were willing to provide. Many black Catholics in the young United States had been baptized while enslaved. And many Catholic slaves were owned by communities of consecrated men and women. Prior to the Civil War, religious orders and other institutes that owned slaves included the Sisters of Charity at Emmitsburg (who had been founded by Saint Elizabeth Ann Seton), the Ursulines, and the Religious of the Sacred Heart of Jesus. Some of the slaves owned by Catholic congregations suffered physical and emotional abuse at the hands of sisters, brothers, and priests. Others experienced relatively humane conditions.[21]

---

20  Mary Alice Chineworth, O.S.P., "Her Oblates Remember Elizabeth Lange: 1784–1882", *Sisters Today* 53, no. 9 (1982): 520–21.

21  Kelly L. Schmidt, "The Pervasive Institution: Slavery and Its Legacies in U.S. Catholicism", *American Catholic Studies Newsletter* 49, no. 1 (2022): 12–14.

Many black Catholic girls, enslaved and free, who grew up around consecrated women desired to become sisters themselves but were denied the opportunity because of their race. This was the case with those who had hoped to join the Religious of the Sacred Heart of Jesus, of which Saint Rose Philippine Duchesne was a sister. Duchesne herself was open to letting them join as coadjutors engaged only in servile functions for the order, but even this plan was rejected by the saint's superiors.[22]

The history of race-based exclusions from Catholic institutes helps us appreciate all the more the story of Mother Lange—whose cause for beatification is open—and that of another black Catholic woman, Eliza Nesbit, who was born around 1814 to enslaved parents owned by the French-born bishop of Louisiana. Nesbit was sold by the bishop as a child and ended up with the Religious of the Sacred Heart of Jesus in Missouri. A group of sisters then took Nesbit back to Louisiana when they were establishing a convent in the parish of Saint Michael's south of Baton Rouge. Eventually, Nesbit attempted to join the order but was rejected due to her race and status as a slave.

Yet Nesbit remained committed to dedicate her life radically to God as she believed He was asking of her—to the point that, years later when no longer enslaved, she received permission to recommit herself annually, with a public vow, as a Sister of Charity of the Sacred Heart. This was not the same thing as becoming fully professed as a nun. But Nesbit was a pioneer for other black American Catholics who desired to respond to callings from God that were especially difficult in the climate of racial discrimination.[23]

Pioneering, too, were the Sisters of the Holy Family established in New Orleans in 1842. They had set up a school for

---

22  Ibid., 18.
23  Ibid.

girls by 1850. Its founding members all had African ancestry: Henriette de Lille, whose father was French and whose
mother had black ancestors; Juliette Gaudin, who was from
Cuba and was Afro Haitian; and Josephine Charles, who
was African American. Wearing simple blue dresses as their
habit, the women ran an orphanage and a school for slaves
with assistance from a racially mixed group of donors. Later
on, the sisters took over teaching responsibilities at various
parochial schools in New Orleans, many of them attended by
poor black children. The congregation remains active today in
several states.

De Lille, whose cause for beatification is open, may eventually, along with Lange and other black Catholic women, join
the ranks of Elizabeth Ann Seton, Frances Xavier Cabrini, and
Katharine Mary Drexel as American women honored as saints.
Another black woman who may eventually be canonized is
Thea Bowman, whose story, as we will see in the next chapter, is tied to the American fight for racial desegregation. That
fight would not take place, however, until after a devastating
era of world wars and the emergence of totalitarian regimes
that severely tested the Church's members around the world.

## Chapter 6

# The Era of World Wars, Totalitarianism, and the Global Church

On June 28, 1914, the devoutly Catholic heir to the Austro-Hungarian imperial throne, Archduke Franz Ferdinand of Austria, was assassinated with his wife, Sophie of Hohenberg, by a Bosnian-Serb nationalist in Sarajevo, the capital of Bosnia-Herzegovina, which had recently been absorbed into the Austro-Hungarian Empire. This assassination sparked a worldwide conflict that some called *the war to end all wars*, but which is remembered as the First World War. Lasting until late 1918, this war resulted in some nine million soldiers' deaths in combat and about ten million civilians' deaths from the effects of war, including the Armenian genocide in the Ottoman Empire. Those wounded and scarred by the war numbered in the tens of millions.

During this conflict, three shepherd children in a city called Fátima in Portugal experienced visions of an angel and the Blessed Virgin, whom they described as "a lady more brilliant than the sun". These children—Lúcia dos Santos and her cousins Francisco and Jacinta Marto—were given the message, among others, that prayer, especially the Rosary, would put a stop to the Great War. The lady also told the children, however, that another terrible war was on the horizon and that there was an urgent need for Russia, in particular, to convert and be consecrated to her Immaculate Heart.

Not long after the final apparition of Our Lady of Fátima in 1917, Russia underwent a revolution that brought to power a deadly Communist regime that was in place until 1991. The world also suffered another cataclysmic war from 1939 to 1945. Casualties of the Second World War, numbering in the tens of millions, included some six million Jewish men, women, and children slaughtered in Nazi death camps, which was about two-thirds of Europe's entire Jewish population. Alongside such horrors engineered by Nazi Germany, Communist regimes murdered as many as 94 million people in the twentieth century.[1] Furthermore, since 1920, when Soviet Russia became the first country to legalize abortion, hundreds of millions of unborn children have been sacrificed to twentieth-century idols—more than 63 million in the United States alone since 1973.

The Church has struggled to witness effectively in such a world, given how caught up in it her members have been. Where she has been a source of light, comfort, and courageous striving for holiness rather than mediocrity, egoism, or worse, her women have been in the vanguard alongside countless good and brave men. In this final chapter, we will encounter some of these Catholic women whose stories help us see both what the Church has suffered and what she has given to the world since the era of World War I.

### Ordinary Catholic women in the era of the First World War

On the eve of World War I, Catholic women all over the world were busy with countless responsibilities for their families, parishes, religious communities, and wider societies. We know a great deal about even the most ordinary among them because numerous records survive, including letters and

---

1   Stéphane Courtois et al., *The Black Book of Communism: Crimes, Terror, Repression*, trans. Jonathan Murphy and Mark Kramer (Cambridge, MA: Harvard University Press, 1999).

journals written in their own hands since women's literacy and educational opportunities had increased dramatically by that point.

One such woman was Élisabeth Arrighi Leseur, a middle-class Frenchwoman married to a physician named Félix Leseur. She kept a diary on spiritual matters after her husband began publicly promoting atheism in Paris. Her husband's antireligious activities made her even more devout, and she prayed continuously for her husband's conversion, especially after she fell sick in 1907 at age forty.

After Élisabeth died of cancer seven years later, grief-stricken Félix was annoyed to find a message she left him that predicted he would become not just a Catholic but a priest. He responded to this in a strange way, visiting the shrine at Lourdes in the hope of proving that accounts of people's miraculous healing by its waters were lies. Unexpectedly, Félix experienced a conversion and did enter the priesthood. He eventually had his wife's journal published and became well known as a retreat leader, later influencing a young American priest named Fulton Sheen.

A French contemporary of the Leseurs who also converted—but only after being mired for years in the modern world's increasing decadence—was Anne-Marie Chassaigne. Better known by her stage name, Liane de Pougy, she fell into a life of promiscuity, prostitution, and drug use as a dancer and actress at the Folies Bergère nightclub in Paris. Eventually, Pougy settled into a respectable marriage. But the great turning point in her life was the death of her son in World War I. This hit her hard, and she unexpectedly found consolation in the Catholic faith and volunteer work, assisting poor children with birth defects along with her husband. In time, Pougy and her husband moved to Lausanne, Switzerland, where they encountered a community of Dominican friars. After repenting of her sins, Pougy became a

Dominican tertiary as a widow and was called Sister Anne-Marie in her final years.

Across the Atlantic, the millions of ordinary Catholic women in the United States on the eve of World War I included Julia Greeley, an elderly black woman who had been born into slavery in Hannibal, Missouri, around 1833. As a girl, she had experienced the horrors of slavery. At only five, her right eye was disfigured while watching her mother get whipped by their master. After emancipation, Greeley worked hard to make a dignified life for herself and impoverished people she encountered.

Upon moving to Denver in her midforties, Greeley worked as a cook and nanny for a wealthy widow named Julia Pratt Dickerson, who introduced her to Catholicism. After deciding to become Catholic herself, Greeley was baptized in 1880 and became a daily Mass attendee. She worked for more wealthy families and was frugal with her pay. She then used her savings to assist the poor whom she met in the streets, encouraging devotion to the Sacred Heart of Jesus. Eventually she became a lay Franciscan.

By the early twentieth century, Greeley was a beloved Catholic philanthropist. After she died on June 7, 1918, several months before the end of World War I, the Jesuits at Loyola Chapel in Denver allowed her body to lie in repose before the altar—the first time they bestowed that honor on a deceased layperson. Almost a century later, her remains were reinterred in Denver's Cathedral Basilica of the Immaculate Conception. Her cause for canonization is open.

Many new institutes of consecrated life were founded and nurtured by women in the second half of the nineteenth century and beginning of the twentieth. These included the Oblate Sisters of Saint Francis de Sales, founded by Saint Leonie Aviat, who were devoted to guiding working-class young women toward lives of virtue and Christian witness in their uprooted, urban circumstances. In Spain, Saint Genoveva Torres Morales founded the Congregation of the Sacred Heart of Jesus and the Holy Angels, which aided homeless, poor, and abandoned women. In Germany and France, the Daughters of the Divine Redeemer, founded by Blessed Alphonse Maria Eppinger, focused on educating very young children and nursing the poor and the sick. Eventually they staffed the teaching hospital at the University of Würzburg and established communities in the United States and Tanzania.

When World War I started, this congregation's general superior, Maria Helene Müller, converted buildings into military hospitals run by the sisters and permitted some women under her authority to serve as nurses on the war's brutal Western Front.[2] In the meantime, her biological sister Caroline, who had immigrated to the United States, was serving the Church in a different way: by raising a brood of working-class Catholic children in New York City and praying patiently for her Lutheran husband's conversion, which eventually occurred in 1930, fifty years into her marriage. The Müller sisters' strong faith—and a pair of cherished Rosary beads belonging to Caroline in her final years—were passed on through several generations, including to Caroline's great-great-granddaughter, the author of this book.

Remarkable contributions by ordinary Catholic women in this period are still coming to light thanks to researchers engaged with the subject. For example, we now know that a group of nuns labored long hours at the Vatican Observatory, contributing knowledge about the locations and brightness of 481,215 stars for an international astronomical project, the 254-volume Astrographic Catalogue of all the known stars in

---

2     Erik Soder von Güldenstubbe, *Congregation of the Sisters of the Holy Redeemer: Past and Present* (Würzburg: Congregation of the Sisters of the Holy Redeemer, 2009), 53.

the universe. These women—essentially working as human computers for publicly credited male scientists—did not do this for fame. But recently their identities were discovered by the Jesuit director of the Vatican Observatory, who publicized them: Regina Colombo, Concetta Finardi, Luigia Panceri, and Emilia Ponzoni. They were all professed as Sisters of the Holy Child Mary.[3]

In the years leading up to World War I, more opportunities opened for women to pursue higher learning and even to teach at the university level. With many young men leaving their professional posts during the war, such opportunities multiplied.

Among the women who benefited from this was one of the most famous women of the modern Church. She achieved a great deal, intellectually and spiritually, before suffering a tragic fate during what many people at the end of World War I believed would never afflict humanity again: another global war that killed millions.

## Edith Stein, philosopher, Jewish convert to Catholicism, and victim of Nazism

A baby girl was born on October 12, 1891, in the city of Breslau in what was then Germany, but which is today in Poland. She was born into a large Orthodox Jewish family, and her name was Edith Stein.

Stein lost her father when she was very young. Her strong-willed mother was determined to see her daughters and sons become educated and have good futures. Stein was thus encouraged to read a lot and think critically. Bright and

---

3    Carol Glatz, "Mapping with the Stars: Nuns Instrumental in Vatican Celestial Survey", *National Catholic Reporter*, April 30, 2016, www.ncronline.org/blogs/eco-catholic/mapping -stars-nuns-instrumental-vatican-celestial-survey.

curious, she went in a different direction with this than her devoutly Jewish mother expected: at thirteen, she renounced Judaism in favor of atheism.

In 1911, Stein enrolled at the local university in Breslau, which had been open to women for a decade. She was introduced there to the work of a German philosopher, Edmund Husserl, who was based at the University of Göttingen about 390 miles away. Stein transferred there to study with him. This was on the eve of World War I. She became devoted to Husserl's philosophical school, phenomenology, which focused on human consciousness and the concrete objects that humans experience, rather than on the nature of being.

As young men in Göttingen left for the war, Stein proved so talented that Husserl took her on as a doctoral student. In 1916, she received her PhD in philosophy, joining only a handful of other women in Germany who had earned doctorates. More remarkably, Husserl asked Stein to join him on the faculty at the University of Freiburg, where he had taken up a new position.

Stein faced discrimination at Freiburg, however, as both a woman and a Jewish person. Her colleagues did not promote her beyond a junior position and rejected some of the research she was doing after her doctoral dissertation work in a postdoctoral project.

In the meantime, Stein encountered Catholicism as an intellectual and religious tradition and over time became more attracted to it. In 1921, she read Teresa of Avila's autobiography, which profoundly moved her. Shocking her colleagues, who were generally irreligious, she was baptized into the Church on January 1, 1922. Soon after, she resigned from her position at Freiburg and became a teacher at a Dominican-run girls' school in the city of Speyer. While there, she translated Saint Thomas Aquinas' *De Veritate* into German and threw herself into other Catholic philosophical works.

In 1932, when she was forty, Stein took up a new position at the Institute of Scientific Pedagogy in Münster. But Adolf Hitler and the Nazis were taking over Germany at that time, and she soon had to step down because of anti-Jewish legislation. Stein decided at this point to follow in Teresa of Avila's footsteps and become a Discalced Carmelite. She entered a convent in Cologne, Germany, and took the religious name Teresa Benedicta of the Cross.

As a nun, Stein continued to work on her philosophical projects. However, four years into her time as a Carmelite, the situation in Germany had become so bad for Jewish people that she was moved to a convent in the Netherlands in the hope that this would protect her from banishment to a work camp or worse. While there, she wrote a phenomenological study of Saint John of the Cross and his "science of the Cross".

In the Netherlands, Stein led her fellow Carmelites in reflections such as the following, on the theme of the marriage of Christ the Lamb:

> Just as the Lamb had to be killed to be raised upon the throne of glory, so the path to glory leads through suffering and the cross for everyone chosen to attend [His] marriage supper.... The spouse whom [the Carmelite] chooses is the Lamb that was slain. If she is to enter into eternal glory with Him, she must allow herself to be fastened to His cross.[4]

Stein's commitment to suffering with Christ was tested severely less than two years after she wrote this. Her life was endangered after the Dutch Catholic bishops spoke out against anti-Semitic policies. This enraged Hitler, who ordered the arrest of non-Aryan Catholics in the Nazi-occupied

---

4    *The Collected Works of Edith Stein*, ed. L. Gelber and Michael Linssen, O.C.D., trans. Waltraut Stein, vol. 4, *The Hidden Life: Essays, Meditations, Spiritual Texts* (Washington, DC: ICS Publications, 1992), 99.

Netherlands. Stein was arrested with her biological sister Rosa, who had also become Catholic and a Carmelite tertiary. They were sent to Auschwitz in Poland and died in a gas chamber just a few days later on August 9, 1942, along with countless other Jewish people. Edith was not yet fifty-one. Rosa was eight years older. Survivors of that death camp testified later that during the short time she was there, Stein was compassionate, assisting other sufferers.

When Stein was canonized in 1998, controversy arose because Pope John Paul II declared her a martyr and confessor. Some objected that she was killed because of her Jewish ancestry, not for her Catholic faith. But the Church's view is that she was killed partly because of the Dutch bishops' condemnation of Nazi anti-Semitism and so died—as both a Christian martyr and confessor—in connection to this teaching of the bishops. Her sister Rosa, while not yet beatified, would also appear to be a martyr and confessor according to this same reasoning.

### Catholic women who resisted Nazism

Edith Stein is not the only Catholic woman honored as a martyr who perished at Nazi hands. The Church has beatified, for example, eleven Polish nuns—all of them Sisters of the Holy Family of Nazareth in the city of Nowogródek—who were executed with machine guns by officers of the Nazi secret police on August 1, 1943.

Blessed Marianna Biernacka, a Polish woman living in a Belarusian farming village, was shot by German soldiers on July 13, 1943. Biernacka, who was about fifty-four, asked the soldiers to kill her instead of her pregnant daughter, her unborn grandchild, and her son-in-law. The soldiers accepted the exchange. Additionally, Blessed Teresa Bracco of Savona, a young Italian woman, was strangled and shot to death by an angry German soldier who tried to rape her on August 28, 1944. Like several young martyrs of the early Church—to whom Bracco had an active devotion—she fought the soldier partly to defend her virginity.

Blessed Sára Salkahazi was a Hungarian member of a congregation called the Sisters of Social Service, whose foundress, Margit Slachta, was the first woman elected to the Hungarian parliament. Salkahazi was killed on December 27, 1944, by pro-Nazi Hungarian officers. She had been leading others in the national Catholic Women's Association she had founded in hiding hundreds of Jewish people in buildings around Budapest.[5]

Also courageous were Blessed Maria Antonina Kratochwil and Blessed Maria Restituta Kafka. Kratochwil was a member of the School Sisters of Notre Dame in the Kresy region of Soviet-occupied Poland when the Nazis took control of it. After suffering persecution from the Soviets, who forbade consecrated people from wearing their habits, Kratochwil and her sisters suffered more under the Nazis. They were thrown into a prison where many Jewish people were also being kept. Kratochwil tried at one point to stop some of the Gestapo's brutal treatment of Jewish women there. This earned her a beating by an officer. Although released from prison, sixty-one-year-old Kratochwil died from her injuries on October 2, 1942.

Kafka was a Franciscan Sister of Christian Charity of Czech background who had grown up in Vienna and worked as a nurse at Lainz Hospital in the Austrian capital and later in the town of Mödling. She became a respected surgical nurse. When Austria joined Nazi Germany in 1938, Kafka,

---

5    Jonathan Luxmoore, "Catholic Priests, Nuns Were among Those Killed by Nazis", *Crux*, May 10, 2020, https://cruxnow.com/church-in-europe/2020/05/catholic-priests-nuns-were-among-those-killed-by-nazis.

who was in her midforties, was outspoken against the Third Reich. Even after being ordered by the Nazis to stop, she maintained Christian practices in her hospital, treating all patients humanely and displaying crucifixes on the walls. She was arrested for opposing the Nazis and was guillotined on March 30, 1943—but not before penning these words: "It does not matter how far we are separated from everything, no matter what is taken from us: the faith that we carry in our hearts is something no one can take from us. In this way we build an altar in our own hearts."[6]

Some Catholic women who fought against Nazism survived World War II. Blessed Enrichetta Alfieri was an Italian Sister of Charity of Saint Jeanne-Antide Thouret who worked for the resistance in Milan. She was arrested for espionage, but ecclesiastical officials secured her release. Zofia Kossak-Szczucka was born into an artistic Polish family and was a famous writer by her early thirties. On the eve of the war, she was made a laureate of the Polish Academy of Literature. Once the Nazis invaded Poland in 1939, she joined the resistance as an underground newspaper editor and founded the Front for the Rebirth of Poland, an anti-Nazi Catholic organization.

In 1942, when Jewish people began to be deported from the Warsaw Ghetto to death camps, Kossak-Szczucka founded the Provisional Committee to Aid Jews with another Catholic activist, Wanda Krahelska-Filipowicz. They helped some Polish Jews escape extermination by the Nazis. Kossak-Szczucka was eventually arrested and sent to Auschwitz, but when the Nazis realized who she was, they returned her to Warsaw and sentenced her to death—a fate she escaped during the Warsaw Uprising, thanks to the Polish underground. After surviving the war, she also resisted the Communist regime that

---

6   "The Cross of Christ versus the Swastika of Hitler", *L'Osservatore Romano*, March 6, 2013.

was imposed upon her country. She died in 1968 at the age of seventy-eight.

It should be noted that numerous Catholics did *not* oppose the Nazis. In fact, when the Nazis came to power in Germany and other countries absorbed into the Third Reich, it was with considerable complicity among Mass-going Catholics. This was due partly to the complicity of many German Catholic bishops. For a time in the early 1930s, Pope Pius XI and his secretary of state, the future Pope Pius XII, believed they could reason with Hitler, with whom they worked out a concordat. Although the Nazis agreed in this treaty to protect the Church in Germany, the Third Reich almost immediately began shutting down Catholic schools and the Catholic press and targeting the Church in other ways.

Few ranking churchmen opposed Hitler bravely until the Americans got involved in World War II and the tide began turning against the Nazis. Many ordinary Catholics in Germany who were horrified by the treatment of Jewish people, the disabled and mentally ill, and other vulnerable groups were afraid to work for the resistance because they felt that their own shepherds in the Church were not with them.

In view of this, it is understandable that many churchmen, in the wake of World War II, began to underscore God's character as a merciful Lord. The Church herself, with the rest of mankind, stood in dire need of His mercy in the dark decades of the twentieth century.

### Faustina Kowalska and the world's growing need for divine mercy

On August 25, 1905, a baby girl was born in the Polish village of Głogowiec. She was the third of ten children born to a poor Polish Catholic peasant couple. They named her Helena, although she is remembered by the Church as the nun and mystic Saint Faustina Kowalska.

When Kowalska was growing up, many Poles were struggling to build their nation after years of domination by Russia, Germany, and Austria. This was even more urgent after the great loss of life and political turmoil during World War I and conflicts with the Ukrainians and the new Soviet Union in subsequent years. Amid all this and the rise of an authoritarian regime in Poland, young Kowalska lived an ordinary life. She went to school, started a job as a housekeeper at age sixteen, and enjoyed social events with friends.

As a teenager, Kowalska developed a strong desire to become a nun, but her parents opposed this. Then, while attending a dance in 1924, she experienced a vision of the suffering Christ as her companions enjoyed the convivial atmosphere. In the vision, Christ asked her sternly, "How long will you keep putting me off?" Shaken by this, she hurried to a nearby church and resolved to become a nun.[7]

Kowalska had difficulty gaining admission into a convent, however. Several congregations turned her down because she was poor and only minimally educated. Finally, one in Warsaw accepted her: the Congregation of the Sisters of Our Lady of Mercy, who assisted girls who had fallen into difficult economic and moral circumstances. Kowalska could not enter the community, however, until she had saved enough money from her job as a servant to afford the entrance fee.

She entered the community on April 30, 1926—twelve days before a deadly military coup overthrew Poland's fragile, young democratic government and led to the authoritarian Sanation regime. She was twenty, and she received the religious name Sister Maria Faustina of the Blessed Sacrament from her superiors.

---

7   Paul Kengor, "Keep Your Eyes on Poland", *Crisis Magazine*, March 3, 2022, https://crisis magazine.com/opinion/keep-your-eyes-on-poland.

Faustina completed her novitiate in 1928 and spent time over the next few years in three convents: the one in Warsaw, another in Vilnius, and a third in Płock. She spent part of that time serving other sisters as a cook.

At Płock, after she had suffered a bout of illness, Faustina began to experience mystical visions of Christ. The first occurred on February 22, 1931. Christ appeared in a radiant form, wearing a white robe with rays of light of red and pale colors streaming out from the area of His heart. He warned Faustina that the last days were approaching. He said, "Mankind will not enjoy peace until it turns with confidence to my mercy." He also instructed her to have an image painted of how He looked to her in the vision and to have it inscribed with the words, *Jesus, I trust in you.* He added,

> I desire that this image be venerated, first in your chapel, and throughout the world. I promise that the soul that will venerate this image shall not perish. I also promise victory over [its] enemies already here on earth, especially at the hour of death. I Myself will defend it as My own glory.... Let the sinner not be afraid to approach Me. The flames of mercy are burning Me—clamoring to be spent; I want to pour them out upon these souls.[8]

Faustina recorded these words in a diary that she kept. We learn from her diary, too, that the other sisters at Płock did not respond favorably to her accounts of her visions. It was not until she was in Vilnius again that she met with encouragement regarding the mission Christ was asking of her. Much of this was owed to her new spiritual director, Father Michael Sopoćko. Sopoćko urged Faustina to submit to a psychiatric

---

8    David Michael Lindsey, *The Woman and the Dragon: Apparitions of Mary* (Gretna, LA: Pelican Publishing, 2000), 320.

evaluation; after she passed it, he found an artist to paint Christ as she had earlier seen him. The artist was the Polish realist painter Eugeniusz Kazimierowski.

Faustina was very pleased with Kazimierowski's Divine Mercy image. Father Sopoćko helped her promote it, displaying it at Mass and preaching on the theme of divine mercy. Faustina then attempted to be released from her religious congregation so that she could start her own institute devoted to the mission Christ gave her, but her request was denied. She also became sick with tuberculosis.

Faustina continued to experience visions. Among them was a terrifying one of Hell and the punishments different kinds of unrepentant sinners suffer there. Some of her visions contained messages from Christ regarding regimes in her time that had been embracing atheistic ideologies. One such regime was Soviet Russia, which by then had caused untold human suffering by means of evils such as a state-engineered terror famine that killed as many as five million Ukrainians.

Sister Faustina did not live to learn of more horrors to come in various countries. She died on October 5, 1938, at age thirty-three—the same age as Christ Crucified. This was less than a year before Poland was invaded by the armies of both Hitler's Germany and Stalin's Soviet Union, events that sparked the most destructive war human beings had ever inflicted on one another.

### Catholic women who resisted Communist regimes

The Hell on earth that was Soviet-era Communism descended upon Poland and many other countries at the end of World War II, when Stalin's Red Army, after helping to defeat the Nazis, remained in Eastern Europe and began terrorizing local populations. The Soviets were also able to see puppet governments, controlled from Moscow, installed in various Eastern European capitals.

The Red Army and other Communist agents targeted Catholic priests and nuns in many places. Lay Catholics also perished at the hands of Soviet agents. This happened to a nineteen-year-old Lithuanian named Elena Spirgevičiūtė on January 4, 1944. Four men—one of whom was later honored in Moscow for his "heroism"—broke into her home in the city of Kaunas, shot her aunt, raped her mother in front of her, and tried to coerce her into satisfying them all sexually. When she refused, she was shot dead while crossing herself.

As had been true under the Nazis, Christians who stood up against Communist regimes did so at the risk of imprisonment, torture, and sometimes death. Some Catholic women were among those courageous souls.

Under Stalin in Russia, hundreds of Roman Catholic and Eastern Rite Catholic clergymen were among the tens of thousands of Christian priests, monastics, and laypeople who were executed or who died as political prisoners. Also killed were several Dominican nuns, including Catherine of Siena Abrikosova. Abrikosova was from a wealthy Russian family and had attended Cambridge University. She and her husband, Vladimir Abrikosov, converted to Catholicism before the Russian Revolution and agreed eventually that she would become a nun and he would become a Ukrainian Catholic priest. The Communists soon began to scrutinize them. While Father Abrikosov was exiled, Sister (and later Mother) Catherine Abrikosova ended up spending twelve years in Soviet prisons. She died inside Butyrka Prison on July 23, 1936, while suffering from spinal cancer. Her husband, in the meantime, was advocating in Rome on behalf of Soviet dissidents, which he continued doing in his wife's memory until his death in 1966.

Another courageous Catholic victim of Soviet Communism was Camilla Kruszelnicka, a university-educated Third

Order Dominican. In 1933, at age forty-one, she was thrown into the dreaded Solovki special purpose camp, or *gulag*, on an island in the White Sea for holding meetings in her Moscow home, in which she and other Catholics discussed religious topics. Inside the gulag, she fell in love with a man who married her but later informed on her after she tried to contact some Catholic priests. She was executed on October 27, 1937.

Catholic women worked against Communist regimes in many ways in the twentieth century. An American socialite, novelist, and eventual congresswoman and US ambassador to Italy named Clare Boothe Luce became an ardent anti-Communist after her conversion to Catholicism in 1946. She worked against Communism as a diplomat, and in the 1960s, she and her husband, Henry Luce, the editor of *Time* magazine, helped fund Cuban exiles' activities against Fidel Castro's revolutionary regime. In Australia and Hong Kong, a convert named Audrey Gladys Donnithorne, who spent her earliest years in China with her Quaker missionary parents, assisted refugees from Communist Vietnam and provided support as well to the underground Church in China. She did the latter with the blessing of Cardinal Joseph Zen. In the meantime, she also became a noted economist. Her most famous work, *China's Economic System*, was published in 1967.

## Women of the modern Catholic Renaissance

Donnithorne became Catholic in 1943 while residing in the United Kingdom during World War II. At this time, a Catholic intellectual and artistic Renaissance was flowering in England, other parts of Europe, and the United States. Donnithorne became friends, for example, with another young convert, the Irish-born analytic philosopher Elizabeth Anscombe, who became famous for her work in philosophy and ethics and her contributions to analytical Thomism while on the faculty at Cambridge University.[9]

Just a few of the men associated with this early- and mid-twentieth-century Catholic Renaissance were artists such as Georges Rouault and Maurice Denis, the novelist J. R. R. Tolkien, and the Thomist philosopher Jacques Maritain. Maritain's story shows especially well how Catholic men and women influenced one another's work in this period. His wife, Raïssa Oumansoff Maritain, led him toward the teachings of Aquinas after they had both converted to Catholicism from atheism in Paris in 1906. Raïssa, who was sick most of her life and unable to publish as much as her husband, was nevertheless a noted poet and philosopher in her own right. After her death in 1960, Jacques lovingly presented her powerful spiritual journals to the world in published form. These journals documented ways the two influenced each other intellectually and spiritually.

Another woman of the modern Catholic Renaissance whose legacy is tied to a notable male scholar is Adrienne von Speyr, who lived from 1902 to 1967. She was a physician, scholar, and author of some sixty books on theology and spirituality. Originally from La Chaux-de-Fonds, Switzerland, she spent most of her life in the city of Basel, where she became drawn to Catholicism after her first husband and the father of her two adopted children died at a young age. At this point, she befriended the priest and theologian Hans Urs von Balthasar, who became her spiritual director, dear friend, and intellectual collaborator for many years. Von Balthasar encouraged her entrance into the Church in 1940, resided with her and her second husband for many years, and was as influenced by her in his remarkable career as she was by him.

---

9    Benjamin J.B. Lipscomb, *The Women Are Up to Something: How Elizabeth Anscombe, Philippa Foot, Mary Midgley, and Iris Murdoch Revolutionized Ethics* (Oxford, UK: Oxford University Press, 2022).

The mid-1900s saw a steady entrance of women into universities and fields of advanced research, and Catholic women were among those establishing reputations as fine scholars. One of them was Christine Mohrmann, a Dutch-born medievalist and Latinist who contributed important studies on the evolution of the Latin language in relation to medieval developments in Christian doctrine and liturgical life. Her work on liturgical Latin, including a book she published in English in 1957, is considered today to be the best on the subject.[10] Mohrmann, who lived from 1903 to 1988, was a professor at both Amsterdam University and the Catholic University of Nijmegen.

Catholic women who were notable visual artists in the prewar and interwar period include Edmonia Lewis and Gwen John. Lewis was an American sculptor of African and Native American heritage whose career blossomed in Rome in the second half of the nineteenth century. She was still active as a sculptor in the early twentieth century, first in Paris and then in London, where she died in 1907. Her work was neoclassical in style, and she was commissioned by Catholic patrons to do statues, altarpieces, and other works for churches.

Gwen John, Welsh by birth, studied at the Slade School of Art at the University College London at the end of the nineteenth century. She developed a notable career as a portrait painter in France, which she continued until her death at age sixty-three in 1939. In 1913, she converted to Catholicism while in France after ending a love affair with the sculptor Auguste Rodin. Among her most striking works are portraits of young nuns in full habits of the period.

Another artist of the period was the Englishwoman Caryll Houselander, who lived from 1901 to 1954. Although she

---

10  Christine Mohrmann, *Liturgical Latin, Its Origins and Character: Three Lectures* (Washington, DC: The Catholic University of America Press, 1957).

was an accomplished painter and engraver of sacred themes, as seen in her 1955 publication *The Stations of the Cross*, she is better known as a writer. One of many books she wrote, *This War Is the Passion*, published during World War II, helped her contemporaries find meaning in the suffering they experienced due to the war. The English priest and theologian Ronald Knox found much value in her work.

Houselander never married after having her heart broken by the British spy Sidney Reilly. She later developed a counseling practice, helping patients cope with various traumas. Her capacity for helping others, including her contemporaries in a war-torn society, was rooted in her mystical prayer life and elicited reflections such as the following, from her book *The Reed of God*: "The modern world's feverish struggle for unbridled, often unlicensed, freedom is answered by the bound, enclosed helplessness and dependence of Christ—Christ in the womb, Christ in the Host, Christ in the tomb."[11]

Catholic women who authored celebrated works of literature in this same period include the brilliant and original Gertrud von Le Fort, a German novelist, poet, and essayist who lived a very long life, from 1876 to 1971. Her most famous novel, *The Song at the Scaffold,* is about the Carmelite martyrs of Compiègne. Her nonfiction work on womanhood in Christianity and modern cultural life, *The Eternal Woman*, has also received renewed interest in recent years.[12]

Another author, Nobel-Prize-winning novelist Sigrid Undset, was a Norwegian Danish woman who converted from atheism to Catholicism in 1924 when in her early forties. Her most famous work, the monumental three-part *Kristin Lavransdatter*, was written around that time and was set in

---

11  Caryll Houselander, *The Reed of God: A Spiritual Classic*, rev. ed. (Notre Dame, IN: Ave Maria Press, 2020), 45.
12  Gertrud von Le Fort, *The Song at the Scaffold: A Novel*, trans. Olga Marx (San Francisco: Ignatius Press, 2011); Gertrud von Le Fort, *The Eternal Woman: The Timeless Meaning of the Feminine* (San Francisco: Ignatius Press, 2010).

medieval Norway. *Kristin Lavransdatter*'s protagonist is a flesh-and-blood woman who struggles with temptation and sin and rivals characters created by the likes of Tolstoy and Dostoevsky. Undset published many works, including other fiction books and nonfiction articles, and advocated for the Jews of Europe in articles and speeches. She produced some of her writing in New York City, where she and her son lived as exiles during the Nazi occupation of Norway. After the war, she returned to Norway, where she died in 1949 at age sixty-seven.

One of the most famous writers of the twentieth century was the American Flannery O'Connor, who spent her whole life— from 1925 to 1964—in her home state of Georgia. Devoutly Catholic, O'Connor often attended daily Mass, and her writings—two novels, thirty-one short stories, and many essays— reflect her Catholic worldview, as well as her southern outlook, in creative ways. She helped develop the Southern Gothic sub-genre of fiction. Sadly, she suffered from lupus, which cut her life and career short. She died at the young age of thirty-nine.

### Catholic women and the American fight for racial desegregation

O'Connor, who in her writing did not shy away from racial problems in the southern United States, lived during a tumultuous period in regard to the fight for black people's civil rights. A major turning point occurred in the spring of 1954, two years after O'Connor's first novel, *Wise Blood*, was published.

On May 17, 1954, the nine justices of the US Supreme Court ruled in favor of Oliver Brown, a welder, and his daughter, Linda. Brown, a black man in Topeka, Kansas, had wished for Linda to attend the public school closest to home, but she was forced to attend a segregated school for black children farther away. With the support of the National Association for the Advancement of Colored People, the Browns joined with other African American families in initiating a class action lawsuit against the local board of education. The case became a federal one, and when the Supreme Court decided that public school officials in Topeka could not forbid black children from attending particular schools because of their race, a historic process of desegregating schools and other institutions across the United States commenced.

After *Brown v. Board of Education* was decided, the governing boards of private schools, including numerous Catholic ones, began to reckon with their own customs of racial segregation. In some places, Catholic churchmen demonstrated leadership. For example, the archbishop of St. Louis, Missouri, Joseph E. Ritter, faced great opposition when he instructed all Catholic schools in his archdiocese to integrate. Some of this opposition came from parents, whom he threatened with excommunication.

Black Catholic laywomen and consecrated women were often on the front lines of desegregation. This was the case when the Jesuits, pressed by black sisters who desired a better education as part of their vocational formation, permitted black students to enroll for the first time at Spring Hill College in Alabama. Additionally, African American sisters from orders such as the Oblate Sisters of Providence—the institute that had been founded by Mary Elizabeth Lange—were the first black students to enroll, in the face of angry opposition, in various Catholic colleges in the United States in the 1940s and 1950s.[13]

In the same period, many women's congregations began the process of racial integration. Many had been traditionally closed to women of color, as we saw in the previous chapter.

Among the women who advanced desegregation within American Catholic institutions was Thea Bowman, who lived

---

13  Shannen Dee Williams, *Subversive Habits: Black Catholic Nuns in the Long African American Freedom Struggle* (Durham, NC: Duke University Press, 2022), 137–38.

from 1937 to 1990. A Catholic convert from Methodism, the daughter of a physician and a schoolteacher in Yazoo City, Mississippi, and the granddaughter of a man who had been born into slavery, Bowman was the first woman of color to become a Franciscan Sister of Perpetual Adoration in La Crosse, Wisconsin. She took part in the desegregation of Viterbo College in the same city in 1958 and later became a leading Catholic liturgist, evangelist, and member of the National Black Sisters' Conference that supports African American women in consecrated life.

Bowman was devoted to serving poor students of color throughout her career and employed the influence she developed over the years, including with many US bishops, to advance this goal. Not long before she died from breast cancer in 1990, she saw one of her final major projects come to life: the establishment of the Sister Thea Bowman Black Catholic Education Foundation. It was set up to provide college scholarships to underserved African American young people, which it has been doing ever since.

## Dorothy Day, foundress of the Catholic Worker movement

For many American Catholics in the twentieth century, dedication to the poor and marginalized became synonymous with the name of a convert who had once been an active Communist. This was Dorothy Day, the foundress of the Catholic Worker movement. Since 1933, this movement's aim has been "to live in accordance with the justice and charity of Jesus Christ" by offering hospitality to poor and unemployed men and women and living in solidarity with them.[14]

---

14 Catholic Worker Movement, "The Aims and Means of the Catholic Worker", https:// catholicworker.org/aims-and-means.

Since her death at eighty-three in 1980, Day has been a figure many in the Church would like to see canonized, and her cause is open in Rome. Given her associations with Communists over the years, others object to the possibility of her canonization. Such polarization testifies, at the very least, to Day's significance in the Church's contemporary history.

Day was born into a middle-class family in Brooklyn, New York, in 1897 but moved around a lot as a girl. Her father worked in the newspaper business, and he brought his wife and five children to San Francisco, Oakland, and Chicago when he took up new positions in those cities.

As Day explained in her autobiography, *The Long Loneliness*, her parents were irreligious, even though they were nominally Episcopalian and had their children baptized. As a child, Day was drawn to Christianity, seeing glimpses of it in her schoolmates' families. She also developed a sense of the kindness of Jesus but did not think of Him as God.[15] But her interests in religion were generally discouraged by influential people in her life, and she was drawn to leftist causes by her young adult years.

After dropping out of college in Illinois, Day moved to New York City and began working for radical newspapers such as the *New York Call*. While there, she also took an active part in protests—for example, on behalf of workers trying to unionize. Most of her friends at this time were socialists, Communists, anarchists, and bohemian writers and artists who opposed religion.

Day had a series of love affairs in her younger years, as well as an abortion that she later regretted terribly. She was also briefly married to a man before taking up with another, Forster Batterham, who was a biologist and activist.

---

15   Dorothy Day, *The Long Loneliness: The Autobiography of the Legendary Catholic Social Activist* (San Francisco: Harper, 1996), 21.

In 1926, when she was twenty-nine and living in Staten Island, Day became pregnant with Batterham's child. This pregnancy led to her conversion. It made her experience a new degree of natural happiness, as she put it, as well as a sense of purpose in becoming a mother. She decided to abandon the disordered lifestyle she was living.

At that point, Day had Catholic neighbors who encouraged her new interest in their faith, and she began attending a parish church nearby. She also studied Catholicism under the guidance of a nun named Sister Aloysia. Day gave birth to a baby girl, whom she named Tamar Teresa after the biblical Tamar and Saint Teresa of Avila, and decided to have her baptized. In 1927, she, too, entered the Church.

In *The Long Loneliness*, Day described how Tamar's birth affected her:

> It was my joy at having given birth to a child that made me do something definite. I wanted Tamar to have a way of life and instruction.... I felt that "belonging" to a Church would bring that order into her life which I felt my own had lacked. If I could have felt that communism was the answer to my desire for a cause, a motive, a way to walk in, I would have remained as I was. But I felt that only faith in Christ could give the answer.... I knew little about the Sacraments, and yet here I was believing.[16]

Day chose Christ knowing it would separate her and her baby from Batterham, who refused to attend his daughter's baptism or to get married. He was dumbfounded by Day's conversion. Although she deeply loved Batterham, she would no longer live in sin with him, so—despite the pain this caused her—she left him and started a new life as a single mother in

---

16  Ibid., 141.

Manhattan. She also began to write for Catholic publications such as *Commonweal.*

The journalist's newfound Catholic faith also alienated her from some of her leftist friends, even as she remained left-wing in her politics. Also, at a time long before the Supreme Court decision *Roe v. Wade*, when radicals were already pressing for the legalization of abortion, Day began to oppose abortion as evil.

The Catholic Worker movement began as a newspaper that Day founded on May 1, 1933. It was the fruit of a new friendship with a French Catholic philosopher and activist, Peter Maurin, who promoted solidarity with the working classes and critiqued social and economic problems from a Gospel-based perspective. Day came to believe that social relationships could be rearranged in a radically egalitarian way as the fruit of recognizing Christ in every neighbor. To practice what she was preaching, she turned her newspaper building in New York's East Village into a hospitality house where food and shelter were offered to hungry and migrant workers displaced by the Great Depression.

The Catholic Worker house and newspaper sparked a movement. Many Catholics followed Day's example and promoted her ideas in their neighborhoods. In 1952, her autobiography was published, sharing the story of her conversion and her understanding of how Catholicism related to her social causes. Day followed up in 1963 with *Loaves and Fishes*, which went into detail about the Catholic Worker movement. Day led the movement until her death in 1980 at age eighty-three.

### Teresa of Calcutta and the Missionaries of Charity

Internationally, the modern Catholic woman who became most identified with the causes of fighting poverty and caring for the most marginalized was a religious sister laboring in India who hailed from southeastern Europe. Known for much of her life as Mother Teresa, she founded the Missionaries of Charity, probably the most famous religious order in the world today.

Guided firmly by her traditional Catholic faith, Mother Teresa was also a very modern woman. We can see this both in how global her experience of the Church was and in how global an impact she had within her lifetime, partly through the medium of mass communication.

Long before she was famous, Mother Teresa was known as Anjezë Gonxhe Bojaxhiu. Born on August 26, 1910, in Skopje, Macedonia, Anjezë grew up in a Kosovar Albanian Catholic family while living initially under the rule of the Islamic Ottoman Empire and eventually—after the difficult period of the Balkan Wars and World War I—under a repressive Yugoslavian regime that would fall to the Nazis.

Anjezë developed a desire by age twelve to become a missionary in India. After traveling to Ireland at the opposite end of Europe when she was eighteen, she joined the Sisters of Loreto, the same institute that had been founded centuries earlier by the controversial Mary Ward. Her intent in choosing an Irish community was to learn English during her novitiate, which she hoped would help her become a missionary in British-colonial India. Indeed, she was sent to India in 1929, before she was twenty. She learned the Bengali language and taught in a mission school near her convent in eastern Calcutta. Upon completing her religious formation in this setting, she made her final profession in 1937, choosing the name Teresa in honor of Thérèse of Lisieux.

Teresa soon became disillusioned with her work in the convent school, where she was appointed as the headmistress. She was horrified by the level of poverty that many in India suffered, especially those regarded in the Hindu caste system as "untouchables", or people with whom those of the higher caste should not mingle because their professions made them "unclean". This included, for example, those who engaged in sanitation work, fished or worked with cattle, or did laundry for a living.

A turning point for Teresa came in the mid-1940s. In 1943, a severe famine hit and many Indians began to suffer extreme poverty and starvation. And in 1946, violence in Calcutta between Muslims and Hindus increased, adding to the misery many suffered. After praying about the matter on a retreat in 1946, Teresa wondered whether she should leave the Sisters of Loreto, who catered to well-to-do girls in their school, so that she could freely serve the poor, sick, and dying.

After much discernment, and after experiencing a profound mystical encounter with Christ that fortified her will, Teresa left the Sisters of Loreto and started her own institute, the Missionaries of Charity, who were approved by Rome in 1950. She and the initially small group of women wore white habits with blue stripes, draped like saris so they could blend in with Indians in the streets of Calcutta.

To facilitate her work among the poor, Mother Teresa, as she was now called, applied for Indian citizenship since India had just become an independent nation, breaking from the British Empire. She also received medical training at a hospital in Patna. She then spent time working in slums in Calcutta and started a school for poor children. Some Indian officials found her work to be disruptive, given some of the long-standing prejudices in the country against the untouchables.

After experiencing the difficulties of her new ministry, Teresa was tempted to give up and return to the Sisters of Loreto. But she and the Missionaries of Charity persevered and became ever more dedicated to their work of giving "whole-hearted free service to the poorest of the poor" and spending time among those most marginalized in India, including refugees, the mentally ill, prostitutes, abandoned children, and lepers.

Mother Teresa's congregation grew dramatically after Pope Paul VI granted her permission to expand into other countries, including Venezuela, Italy, Tanzania, and Austria. The order also established a branch for men and another for contemplative women. Mother Teresa believed that the social-justice-oriented work of her order was not in conflict with, but dependent upon, lives fully dedicated to prayer, such as those of contemplatives.

Mother Teresa became globally known in her lifetime thanks to modern mass media. She also traveled beyond India to bring media attention to human suffering in other parts of the world, such as the Middle East in 1982 when she helped rescue thirty-seven children trapped in a hospital during the Siege of Beirut, a conflict between the Israelis and Palestinians. She traveled, too, to Ethiopia when many were starving there.

Mother Teresa received the Nobel Peace Prize in 1979. But she received a lot of criticism, too, as she was outspoken against abortion and contraception at a time when activists in the West were pushing hard for them and painting the Church as backward for opposing them.

Books were written about Mother Teresa during her lifetime, such as the British journalist Malcolm Muggeridge's *Something Beautiful for God.* Many other books—as well as television shows, newspaper articles, and films—about her and her missionaries have also appeared over the decades. Her journals, published after her death, reveal that she experienced dark nights of the soul and even struggled with faith. One day she wrote, for example, "When I try to raise my thoughts to Heaven—there is such convicting emptiness that those very thoughts return like sharp knives and hurt my very soul."[17]

---

[17] Mother Teresa, *Come Be My Light: The Private Writings of the Saint of Calcutta*, ed. Brian Kolodiejchuk, M.C. (New York: Image, 2007), 187.

Mother Teresa became friends with Pope John Paul II. Sadly, she had a heart attack when visiting him in Rome in 1983. She suffered additional heart problems and illnesses after that but remained in charge of the Missionaries. Mother Teresa died on September 5, 1997, and was given a state funeral by the Indian government in gratitude for the orphanages, hospitals, schools, and hospices that she and her order had established. By that point, greater consciousness had been raised in India about treating certain people as untouchables and the Missionaries of Charity had become a strong international order. Today, they have more than 5,100 members in over 130 countries.[18]

After Mother Teresa died, her cause for canonization opened quickly, and she was canonized in 2016. In 2017, Pope Francis named her as a co-patron—with the Jesuit Francis Xavier—of the Archdiocese of Calcutta. She is also the patron saint of World Youth Day and of the Missionaries of Charity.

### Women of the Church in the Global South

Early during Mother Teresa's time leading the Missionaries of Charity, the bishops of the Church met in Rome for the Second Vatican Council. Missionary work was among the themes they addressed. The Vatican II decree *Ad Gentes*, promulgated in 1965, addressed the Church's missionary identity in new terms: "The pilgrim Church is missionary by her very nature, since it is from the mission of the Son and the mission of the Holy Spirit that she draws her origin, in accordance with the decree of God the Father."[19]

---

18  "Missionaries of Charity, Their Increasing Numbers throughout the World", *Rome Reports*, February 19, 2016, https://www.romereports.com/en/2016/09/02/missionaries-of-charity-their-increasing-numbers-throughout-the-world/.

19  Vatican Council II, Decree on the Mission Activity of the Church *Ad Gentes* (December 7, 1965), no. 2.

*Ad Gentes* also underscored, in stronger terms than past official statements, that charity toward the poor was constitutive to evangelization. Other documents since Vatican II have also stressed the principle of inculturation, by which missionaries live among those they hope to convert, absorbing their ways while making Christianity understandable within their cultures. As we have seen, Mother Teresa and other missionaries, including many women, had understood such things long before bishops put them into solemn words at a council.

The purpose of *Ad Gentes* was not simply to instruct professed missionaries in how to do their work. The bishops understood by the mid-1960s that the world had changed greatly since the previous ecumenical council and that places that had once been heartlands of the Church were falling away from faith and stood in need of evangelization themselves.

Among the important narratives of the twentieth century is the decline, from the 1960s onward, in Mass attendance and vocations to the priesthood and religious life in Europe and North America, or what many call the Global North. At the same time there has been an increase in Mass attendance and vocations in Latin America, parts of Asia, and especially Africa, or what many call the Global South.

At a time when women's religious life sharply declined in Europe and North America, congregations such as the Missionaries of Charity expanded dramatically in India, many African nations, the Philippines, and other non-Western lands. Furthermore, in recent decades, consecrated women from these countries have been sent on missions in the United States, France, Italy, and other countries in the Global North, in the same way that priests and brothers from the Global South are now ministering to Catholics in formerly more Christian lands.

While the Church in the Global South often appears more fervent than that of the Global North, it also faces challenges, including competition from other Christian groups that are winning large numbers of conversions, sometimes from among Catholic populations. There is also great competition in some places between the Church and Islam—competition that has occasionally turned deadly.

The contemporary Church has her martyrs, as did the Church in the eras of totalitarianism, revolutions, the Reformation, and early Christianity. And women of the Church in the Global South are among those martyrs. For example, Leonella Sgorbati, a Consolata Missionary sister originally from Italy, was targeted by Islamist militants in Somalia on September 17, 2006. She was shot in the thigh and the back by two armed men who, following the orders of a Muslim cleric, believed they were honoring Allah and the prophet Muhammad. Sgorbati did not die right away, but one of the bullets hit an artery and she died shortly after being rushed to a local hospital. A witness, Sister Marzia Feurra, said that Sgorbati's last words were "I forgive, I forgive, I forgive."[20] On May 26, 2018, Sgorbati was beatified as a martyr.

Other Catholic women who have lost their lives to Islamic jihadists in the Global South include four Missionaries of Charity who died in Aden, Yemen, on March 4, 2016. On that day, gunmen attacked a facility for the elderly run by the Missionaries, killing sixteen people. The four Missionaries—Sister Anselm from India, Sisters Margherite and Reginette from Rwanda, and Sister Judith from Kenya—were shot execution style. They had prayed earlier that day, "Lord, teach me to be generous. Teach me to serve you as you deserve; to give and not to count the cost, to fight and not to heed the wounds, to toil and not to seek for rest, to labor and not

---

20 "Pope Francis Recognized Sister Leonella Sgorbati as Martyr", *Aleteia*, May 24, 2018, https://www.romereports.com/en/2016/09/02/missionaries-of-charity-their-increasing -numbers-throughout-the-world/.

to ask for reward."[21] They were not the first Missionaries of Charity to be killed in Yemen. Three others—two from India and another from the Philippines—were killed in the city of Hodeidah in 1998.

The stories of countless other courageous and saintly Catholic women of contemporary times could fill many more pages of this book. Entire books have recently been written on figures such as Saint Gianna Molla, the Italian physician who in 1962 refused to allow her fourth child to be aborted in exchange for her own survival of a difficult pregnancy, and Mother Mary Angelica of the Annunciation—better known as Mother Angelica—the American nun who founded the Eternal Word Television Network (EWTN) and an entire international media empire.[22] The remarkable writings of some brilliant, faithful Catholic women, such as Ida Friederike Görres, an author of Austro-Hungarian and Japanese ancestry, who wrote prolifically on themes of Catholic morality, history, and doctrine, are still becoming familiar to readers in America.[23] And the stories of many virtuous twentieth-century women of the Church, like their counterparts in previous eras, still need to be pieced together and written. Some of these women may come to be venerated as saints.

Many readers of this book, too, are admirable women of the Church—or are fathers, brothers, sons, and friends of such women. Some of their stories may also one day be among those "every Catholic should know". But most will live their faith with quiet, unassuming, and unsung courage, sometimes amid great suffering. They can take at least some consolation

---

21  Elise Harris and Alan Holdren, "There's No Question—the Missionaries of Charity in Yemen 'Died as Martyrs'", *Catholic News Agency*, March 6, 2016, www.catholicnewsagency.com/news/33527/theres-no-question-%E2%80%93-the-missionaries-of-charity-in-yemen-died-as-martyrs.
22  Pietro Molla and Elio Guerriero, *Saint Gianna Molla: Wife, Mother, Doctor*, trans. James G. Colbert (San Francisco: Ignatius Press, 2004); Raymond Arroyo, *Mother Angelica: The Remarkable Story of a Nun, Her Nerve, and a Network of Miracles* (New York: Doubleday, 2005).
23  See, for example, Ida Friederike Görres, *The Church in the Flesh*, trans. Jennifer S. Bryson (Providence, RI: Cluny Media, 2023).

in knowing how many other women have gone before them and are praying *for* them and *with* them on the other side of death, in the eternal light of God.

Those prayers include one we have been singing to Mary, the Mother of God, in different languages in the Church on earth for a thousand years:

Hail, Holy Queen, Mother of Mercy,
Our life, our sweetness, and our hope.
To thee do we cry, poor banished children of Eve.
To thee do we send up our sighs,
Mourning and weeping in this valley of tears.
Turn then, most gracious advocate,
Thine eyes of mercy toward us,
And after this, our exile, show unto us
The blessed fruit of thy womb, Jesus.
O clement, O loving, O sweet Virgin Mary,
Pray for us, O holy Mother of God,
That we may be made worthy of the promises of Christ.